Good Times With Old Times

D0836020

Main Street
(Cover Photo)

Its two blocks, bounded by the train station at one end and the highway leading to the Big City at the other, were the community's main artery. Daily we children crossed Main Street to go to school and the post office, passing groups of older men who warmed body and soul on the benches in front of the bank and our store, talking, cracking sunflower seeds, and watching village life go by.

We were sent to its various business establishments to get whatever Mother and Dad needed. To carry a money deposit for Dad up the steep steps of the bank into its silent, high-ceilinged chambers took courage. To bring worn-out shoes to the friendly shoemaker was a small pleasure. During the week we went to Main Street because we had reason to do so.

On Saturday evenings Main Street, usually sluggish, moved into action. The rural population joined local residents for an evening of shopping and visiting on its dimly lit streets. Side attractions included the poolroom, the picture show, a restaurant, or even a Salvation Army street meeting. Perhaps even an occasional drunken brawl. We youngsters tramped its length looking for excitement, for Main Street on Saturday evening was life—the best of life, even if it only consisted of a bottle of pop or a two-cent piece of bubble gum.

—*The Author*

Good Times With Old Times

How to Write Your Memoirs

Katie Funk Wiebe

HERALD PRESS
Scottdale, Pennsylvania
Kitchener, Ontario
1979

Library of Congress Cataloging in Publication Data

Wiebe, Katie Funk.
  Good times with old times.

    1. Autobiography. I. Title.
CT25.W45   808'.066'92   79-12864
ISBN 0-8361-1894-4

GOOD TIMES WITH OLD TIMES
Copyright © 1979 by Herald Press, Scottdale, Pa. 15683
    Published simultaneously in Canada by Herald Press,
    Kitchener, Ont. N2G 4M5
Library of Congress Catalog Card Number: 79-12864
International Standard Book Number: 0-8361-1894-4
Printed in the United States of America
Design: Alice B. Shetler

15 14 13 12 11 10 9 8 7 6 5 4 3 2 1

To
Frieda
Anne
Jack
Susan
who helped
make the
good times
possible

Contents

Foreword

In *Good Times with Old Times* Katie Funk Wiebe reminds older persons that they, their children, and their grandchildren share a common past that can be meaningful to all.

That she feels strongly about her subject is quickly evident when she speaks of the great vacuum in our lives and of the need to establish continuity with the past in order to live more satisfactorily and fully in the future.

Katie Funk Wiebe takes her readers from an I-don't know-how stance to an edge-of-the-chair eagerness to write their own memoirs. Yet she checks this eagerness long enough to advise adequate contemplation and the consideration of purpose, direction, and form.

Her direction regarding research sources is especially helpful. Having followed this route in my own writing, particularly in an escape-from-Russia book, *Louise* (Harold Shaw Publishers), I understand the need for searching every nook and cranny—journals, letters, people, history, maps—for meaningful supportive information. I especially commend her for her attention to intimate detail which makes the examples from her own writing throb with life and emotional appeal.

Though the book provides a logical approach to writing personal memoirs, its value is heightened by its ability to spark a reader's recall of memories from his or her own past. Repeatedly I found myself inundated by memories from my past. They literally tumbled over each other. Experiences I thought I had forgotten came back to me precisely as they had happened, often in living color. I felt myself responding with the same disappointment, joy, sorrow, or anticipation I had experienced when the incident occurred.

And, as the book suggests, I found myself accepting my past for what it was with its failures and successes. As a result I appreciate anew the me that has emerged from these experiences.

When I was doing research for my book *Your Aging Parents: When and How to Help* (Concordia Publishing House), I attended a conference at the Andrus Gerontology Center, University of Southern California. For three days I listened to outstanding gerontologists, psychologists, and social workers address themselves to the problems of filial relationships, particularly the relationship between adult children and their aging parents.

At one session Dr. Carlfred B. Broderick, Professor of Sociology, Director of the Marriage and Family Counseling Center at USC, referred to intergenerational relationships in his own family. One summer he and his wife found themselves at a loss knowing how to help a teenage daughter, restless and indifferent about her future. Quite by chance Dr. Broderick's parents solved their problem. They invited the girl to spend the summer with them in California. She accepted the invitation.

Before long she had become so captivated by tales her grandparents told her about their past, she decided to interview and write biographies about them. In doing so she learned new appreciation for them, for her father, and for herself.

"She knows more about our roots than any member of the family," Dr. Broderick told conferees. "More important, she learned that older people have something important to say."

Anthropologist Margaret Mead frequently asked her students to interview the elderly in their families. This project proved so successful they developed a model guidebook: *How to Interview Your Grandfather.* They explained that they formulated their interview questions simply by assessing what they wanted to know about the past.

And now Katie Funk Wiebe comes along with an inspiring how-to guidebook directed to older persons themselves. It could well have been titled *How to Interview and Write About Yourself.*

I count it a privilege to recommend such a valuable book for use in homes, schools, and public libraries.

Margaret J. Anderson
Turlock, California
September, 1978

Introduction

Good Times with Old Times is an egg with a double yolk. Two books for the price of one. As the subtitle states, one is a how-to-do-it book filled with helpful counsel and encouragement for persons writing memoirs, autobiographies, or simply their stories. The other book is Katie Funk Wiebe's story—a series of mini-portraits of her life from Blaine Lake beyond the North Saskatchewan River to Hillsboro in Kansas. She skillfully uses in bits and pieces her story to illustrate both the fun and the method of writing about one's own experiences.

Perhaps the best of Katie Funk Wiebe's book is left for the last twenty pages where she unfolds one part of her story under the title "You Never Gave Me a Name." But no peeking; save that story for last. Throughout, the whole book is a delightful point and counterpoint of moving back and forth from instructional material to chapters in one person's story. All this insures that the manual or guidebook part of the book does not drag but moves along at a sprightly, entertaining pace.

Telling one's story is, of course, the biblical way of

sharing the truth. The Old Testament is a book of stories, biographies, and the sweeping drama of God's people. Jesus went about telling stories. His followers learned through stories. Just before he was stoned to death Stephen took those last minutes to tell the story of his people. Storytelling is a way of reporting how the Holy Spirit continues to work among us.

Elie Wiesel suggests that perhaps God created man because He loves to tell stories and He needed someone to whom He might tell His stories. I suspect that the Jewish people—probably also Mennonite people—have survived so much persecution because of their gift to remember and to tell stories.

Hence, Katie Funk Wiebe is not simply helping us in some quaint, antiquarian exercise. She is helping us and herself in the quest to be a people, to know God's will, to have a sense of worth as one of God's children. Writing one's memoirs looks like good therapy.

I like what she has to say about the cleansing/renewing values of writing out of one's storehouse of memories:

> For most people writing meaningfully begins with an impelling urge to systematize their philosophy of life, to unravel the muddle of life, to let others know the felt quality of what life has been. . . . As you write, you will soon discover that to accept the past as it was, with all its weaknesses and strengths, is a freeing experience. Once you have owned it as your own, it no longer owns you or controls your feelings. It now belongs to you. You have forgiven as you were forgiven. You can make the past serve you.

The idea for *Good Times with Old Times* appears to have been sparked in Katie Funk Wiebe's mind by a group of her students—a special group of students. In her preface she explains:

> This is a book about writing for people who don't write much, to encourage them to do more. It developed out of a college continuing education class I taught in spring 1975 for 26 men and women sixty years and older. A few were in their eighties. My students were interested in learning to write their memoirs.

She gives an abundance of good counsel for people writing for the fun of it. Her suggestions come in small packages—never so much as to overwhelm one. Her tips are always simple, direct, practical. The suggestions flow forth like this: begin small . . . one step at a time . . . see writing as fun . . . pick an audience to write for . . . tell your story in many stories . . . no moralizing . . . give people names . . . write about critical incidents . . . be specific, concrete . . . avoid pious clichés . . . mention the little people in your life . . . recall strong feelings . . . don't explain too much . . . record facts, but as they affected you . . . use simple, but natural-sounding language . . . blend the world of facts with the world of inner life . . . draw a floor plan of your childhood house.

To illustrate her teaching points she uses little excursions into her life story—for example, on hospitality in the Funk home:

> Dad had to pass the livery barn each evening on the way home from the store where he worked. If he saw a family, particularly with women and small children, planning to bed down in the barn for the night, they ended up at our place, Mennonite or non-Mennonite. They were human be-

ings in need of a bed. Dad often paid the livery stable fee for the travelers' horses as well. "They had no money," was his excuse, and horses had to be liveried. That he had little money either didn't count.

In the memories of our people is a rich lode of ore. For some, there are memories of persecution and flight. For others, the scorn of war years. For others, the shared camaraderie of rural communities. For some, life on the thin margin of survival in the depression. For others, exhilarating experiences on frontiers of church service. For many, a series of conflicts. Every family, every congregation, every community needs persons who can help us remember our stories. Once we know our story we are on the way to self-understanding and spiritual liberation.

I hope that a hundred potential storytellers are inspired by this volume to write their memoirs. The world will be a richer place because of *Good Times with Old Times*.

> *Robert Kreider*
> North Newton, Kansas
> September, 1978

Author's Preface

This is a book about writing for people who don't write much, to encourage them to do more. It developed out of a college continuing education class I taught in spring 1975 for 26 men and women sixty years and older. A few were in their eighties.

My students were interested in learning to write their memoirs. I knew something about writing; they knew something about living. We pooled our resources and talked about many things, such as the value of leaving a written record behind, the best ways to force memory to release its treasure trove, the best types of memories to record, and how to make such writing meaningful. Finally, we discussed what a look at the past can do for writer and reader.

I gave writing assignments at each session. The choice of whether or not to do the assignment was always up to the student. Some came and listened to the discussion; others listened and wrote. Some assignments were only exercises to strengthen writing skills; others were stories which could be incorporated in their memoirs.

In addition to the exercise of drawing a floor plan of an early home (Chapter Two), these assignments required the students:

1. To tell a story about a childhood event.
2. To write a character sketch of some person close to them.
3. To write about an incident which changed the direction of their lives.
4. To write about an inner experience, one which only they were aware of, such as fear, frustration, humiliation, disappointment, joy, and hope.
5. To state an attitude they had held at some time, either favorable or unfavorable, toward some idea, person, or institution—for example, racial prejudice—and to trace the development of this attitude.
6. To explain some of the family, church, and community customs they enjoyed or endured as a child or young person.

The students handed in the assignments, and I read them all. I commented on the papers, usually indicating where a piece of writing could be developed or made clearer. Always I encouraged. During the time we worked together, we never worried about spelling, punctuation, or grammar. Our concern was getting thoughts on paper.

As the class drew to a close, one woman said, "We can't quit now. I've learned so much about myself I didn't know before. Schools should have such courses in their curricula." I wanted to tell her they do. In college such courses are frequently called Freshman English Composition, but the act of writing and college freshmen are frequently mismatched partners.

One student added a thank-you note to her last paper:

Dear Friend and Teacher:

I want to let you know that I enjoyed the memoirs class
very much. Thank you for all your suggestions and also for
the remarks on my handed-in papers. Some of the things
you reminded me of I hadn't thought of, but it all came
back to me. You are the most pleasant teacher I ever had. I
am a slow thinker; things don't come to my mind so quick. I
wish the college would have had something like this years
ago, when my mind was more alert. Now I'm almost 86, but
I still enjoy learning. I will do over a lot of my writing.

In 1977 another student, Mrs. Frieda Suderman,
published a book of her memoirs. *You Just Can't Do
That Anymore* is a delightful account of her growing
years in a large family in the early days of Kansas. Other
students assure me they are still writing. What other
reward could a teacher want?

The material is presented here to encourage individuals to begin writing their memoirs and to give
guidance to groups.

Good writing.

Katie Funk Wiebe
February, 1978

Good
Times
with
Old Times

How to Write Your Memoirs

CHAPTER ONE

Why Write Your Memoirs?

P-sst, Grandpa and Grandma. This is for you.

Mom and Dad, it won't hurt you to listen either.

I've got an idea to help you beat inflation when it comes to gift-giving. Give your children a gift worth hundreds of dollars—but it will only cost you pennies.

What is it?

A part of yourself—in writing. Give them your memoirs.

As my older friends get older, I hear them saying, "I wish I had written down more of my early experiences, so my children would know what it was like to trudge to school two miles each way, to use horses to plow the fields, and to do homework by the light of the kerosene lamp."

Well, it's never too late to start writing, so why not begin now? Say good-bye to weary arches brought on by shopping for plastic toys and matching shirt and sweater sets. Forget about rain slopping in your face, snow melting down your coat collar, or wind snatching the hat from your head. Put your feet into your most comfortable slip-

pers. Find yourself a pen and paper, a well-lighted place
to work, and begin. You'll be doing what grandparents
have done with their children for centuries. Around open
fires outside a simple shelter, or by crackling fireplaces
inside their homes, they told the family stories about the
past. The past belonged to them, the elders. Yet it had to
be conveyed to the next generation to pass on knowledge
and wisdom accumulated by those who had lived before.
Evening after evening, the older generation related story
after story to the younger ones to explain what life had
been—not selecting any particular story or stories, but
telling each one as they recalled it; and then on another
evening, telling it again and adding other details. But the
act of telling was important, so that the next generation
could join hands with the past and learn enough from it
to be able to say, "I know now who I am because I know
what made me." Accepting the past as it was brings
freedom to be in the present.

Young and old are asking today, "Who am I? Where
did I come from? What in my past has made me into the
person I am becoming?" Answers are not readily available because often Grandpa and Grandma live in
California or Kansas, and the children live in Florida or
Illinois. Children don't know where they came from (was
it Colorado or Ontario?), still less, where Grandpa and
Grandma pledged their troth and began a new branch of
the family tree.

One out of three families moves every year; some even
oftener. Some of my middle-aged friends tell me that
twelve to fifteen moves before they settled down permanently is about par for the course. With some families,
with each such move, another little section of the family
root system breaks off and is left behind with the old

davenport which wouldn't sell and the draperies which wouldn't match the decor in the new house. And so, in time, the root system dries up completely. Today's children must find their identity by relating to the neighborhood and school where the family lives for the time being and draw from its shallow springs, set in stainless steel and gleaming porcelain, sufficient strength to affirm to themselves that a life that begins is a life with meaning.

The child with a sense of the past is a child with a sense of destiny. The child with a past from which to draw is a rich child. How well I remember sitting around the oak table with its strawberry-decorated oilcloth covering, listening to my parents talk about times of famine and plenty, about ghosts and God, about birthings and death, in the Ukraine in Russia. They told terrifying stories about cannons in the backyard during the revolution and hunting for lost family members after the war. One man was placed before a firing squad to be shot, but the bullets missed, so he was released.

These stories unconsciously built a bridge for me to a heritage which includes many new beginnings in new locations, both forced and chosen, yet undergirded by faith and courage, suffering and endurance. These stories aroused my imagination. In my mind I pictured my father as a young man of about 25, catching a boat ride down the Dnieper River to find Mother's family, lost during the upheaval caused by the revolution and war. He didn't even know what her family looked like. But gradually the story of that episode is forming as I continue to research books and ask questions of those who were part of this dramatic moment when he found her parents and showed them a picture of his wife—their daughter. "Is my daughter still alive?" asked my mother's mother. Then she cried. Family ties. Strong ones. What in our society makes them so easy to sunder? The pitch of excitement within me can hardly be contained as I piece together the entire long story of this reunion of Mother with her parents and brothers and sisters.

Yet what nurtures the imagination of today's children? Can police and spy thrillers on television do as much for them as family stories out of the past? Can each new backyard patio or school gym provide the same sense of continuity, the same dignity which comes from being secure in one's identity? Can anything but true stories of yesteryear convey what parents and grandparents endured and survived—of what the human spirit is capable of enduring and surviving—so that when our time comes to face difficulty, we too know we can make it?

The black and Chicano people are rapidly recognizing the need to know one's past. With the awakening of a race-consciousness, blacks are insisting their children study black history and culture to give them a better understanding of the present situation. In recent years college curricula have introduced courses in black history and literature. Black spokesmen, such as Langston Hughes and others, realize that if black Americans are ever to discover their identity, they must first retrace the painful road from slavery to their present situation. For they, like everyone else, live in a "stream of history, in part the fulfillment of forces and voices of the past, and in part the fulfillment of forces and voices of the past, and in part the creator and prophet of the future." To live without a knowledge of one's heritage is to live without moorings, a ready target for any ideology and ism. It's like going to high school without having finished grade school.

In Ralph Ellison's short story "Flying Home," a young black flyer crash-lands his plane on a plantation in Alabama during the war years. He, a young educated Northern black, feels repulsed by the ugly, ignorant old Negro field hand who helps him. He wants no part of this old man. Yet, at the end of the story, the young man realizes that part of himself is represented by this simple old man. He discovers an identity which goes beyond mere skin color or race. He and the old man are one, not in culture and place of origin, but because they share the experiences, good and bad, of a common slave heritage.

This kind of identification is more than a cultural bond, strengthened by eating the same foods or wearing the same style of clothing. It is a spiritual link to the experiences of the past which binds one forever together. But only if one wants to be bound together.

You and your children and grandchildren share a common past. But they will never know anything about it unless you share it with them. You can give them this past if you tell them about your fantasies as a child; your fears and blunders as an adolescent; your aspirations, models, and friends as a young adult; and your failures and successes as a more mature person. Although no one should be chained to the past, nor glorify it beyond what it was, you are helped if you know how your thinking today has been affected by past events and ideas and by the leaders who were part of this experience. It is easier to get to where you want to go if you know where you've come from.

Many young people don't know where they're going. So a review of your past could lead them to a reassessment of their values—values which may have been sidestepped and overlooked because no one pointed them out. You can help to identify to a new generation the past acts of God in your life, so that those looking for evidence of God's working today can recognize it in a new social setting.

As you begin to think of writing your memoirs, remember, people frequently take one of two extremes in their attitudes toward the past. For some, digging into their roots in attics and basements of houses and minds causes them to get so deeply involved with their own brand of Americana that their writing is mostly a gawking at strange customs of the past instead of dialogue with it. Their nostalgia trips encourage the revival of old forms and practices: "It was so good when we did it the old way. Surely the old is better than the way it is done today." For some, looking for roots is an escape from facing the problems of the present. They venerate the past but refuse to learn from it.

Others refuse to have anything to do with the past. It's back there. It doesn't count. They kick the ladder away by which they arrived at the present, seeing themselves as self-made persons. They step confidently into the present and turn only to themselves for wisdom and strength. They may as well have walked into a room of mirrors, for all they see is their own image, reflected again and again. Such constant self-reflection and probing may lead to insecurity and frustration, for the past can give them no guidance. The future is nonexistent. The present is self.

But there is a better way. Philosopher Michael Novak writes, "People who are secure in their past and joyful in the present cannot but be hopeful in their future." A balanced approach to the past leads to wholeness. In a time of rapid social change, everyone needs to be related to time, to be connected to his or her origins, to affirm constantly what has made the individual, and learn from it.

Is It Only a Fad?

Is the writing of memoirs, the search for roots, the recovery of the past, only a fad? Not at all, say sociologists. The modern lifestyle has created a vacuum in people's lives through the constant moving from place to place and the present pattern of marrying and divorcing, thereby leaving relatives and heritage far behind in photograph albums and garage sales. The mobile lifestyle lacks continuity. It has gaps. The writing of memoirs closes some of these gaps for the writer and also for the one who reads the finished product. It tells people who they belong to and why. I speak from experience.

I caught my first conscious glimpse of the past when, as a young person, I came upon a genealogy which my paternal grandmother had kept of her father's side of the family. It dated back to 1769. As I copied it for myself, I wondered about the mother who had buried three infants before she was 26, about the young girl with the same name as mine, about the mother who lost six children in infancy and an older one through drowning. What had they thought and felt about life? As I grew older, I feared that my generation would be the last to have a sense of living history and a firm identity established by family history. I had at least this genealogy, this skeleton, but wasn't there more?

I began copying stories my parents had told us children years ago. I knew that as my parents grew older, like my own grandparents whom I never really knew, they would move out of the lives of my children and take with them their stories of sharing, building, hurting, and healing. My children would lose valuable knowledge of their own roots, which in some cases had been prematurely broken off by wars and migrations. They would never know the essence of the human spirit—its ability to bear all kinds of adversities and survive. They would never appreciate pride of being part of a people who knew what they stood for—until they came to North America and were nearly lost in the melting pot.

Many years later, one day I came upon a book of genealogies, lists of people, and details of the wanderings of my forefathers, the Mennonites, from Prussia to Russia.° One entry read:

Family No. 2: Frans Funk 46, Wife Maria 38, Children Frans 17, Johan 15, Eva 10, Helena 8, also Widow Susana Funk, about 58. With 7 horses, 13 head of cattle, 16 sheep, 4 pigs, 1 plow, 2 harrows, 2 wagons, 2 spinning wheels.

My grandmother's book said her forefathers had come to Russia in 1789 from Danzig. These names and dates matched the names and dates in her book. This book now placed them in a specific locality in the Ukraine and gave added information. What a discovery! About two hundred years ago Frans and Maria Funk, born 1769 and 1775 respectively, packed their belongings into two wagons and trekked hundreds of miles to their new

---

°Benjamin Heinrich Unruh. *Die Niederländisch-niederdeutschen Hintergründe der Mennonitischen Ostwanderungen im 16., 18. und 19.* Jahrhundert. Im Selbstverlag. Karlsruhe, Germany: 1955.

home. They were the first links I had found in the long chain of my own history. Dan Rottenberg in *Finding Our Fathers: A Guidebook to Jewish Genealogy* (Random House) writes about the "humbling realization that each of us is merely a link in a chain. We may some day be forgotten, but the contribution we made to the chain, however slight, will always be there, and as long as the chain exists, a piece of us will exist, too." For me it was a sacred moment to know I belonged to that vanished world; yet I could face the future with clearer vision. I had been. I am. Therefore I will be.

The writing of your memoirs may never stop inflation, a strike, or a riot, but it will help your readers, young and old, to understand the gift of their heritage and to feel the ground becoming firmer under their feet. A knowledge of the past will give strength to face an uncertain future. Humankind has always faced difficult odds, but the pathway ahead is surer and clearer if a pattern of faith and courage preceded it, and if this pattern is available for others to read.

So, write your memoirs for your children. But write them also for yourself. To renew acquaintance with the past will be like finding an old friend. You may find aspects of yourself and your past you didn't know existed, aspects you may even have reason to boast about now. A knowledge of your heritage may also bring back memories of idiosyncrasies (at least you thought of them that way) against which you once rebelled. Writing about what has gone before will give you a chance to see your life through eyes that have become wiser and more mellow. Instead of an awkward gangling youth or a timid woman reexamining the frightening but exciting experience of the first swell of love, you are a person who has loved well and long, and who can now hold up this fragile moment to the light of experience and enjoy it once again with a new savor.

There are the other kinds of experiences you will encounter also in your trek into time—the hard and bitter ones. When I was a child, our car sometimes got stuck in mudholes in the dirt road during summer downpours. It took much pushing and pulling to drag it out. Sometimes Dad had to get a team of horses from a nearby farm to accomplish the task. After we were out of the hole, back on more secure ground, my father sometimes went back to look at the hole again, as if to say, "Well, that's one we won't get stuck in again." And we never did, for the next time we traveled that way, the road was dry and graded.

In writing your memoirs, go back and look at the mudholes from a new perspective in time and space, and assign them a fitting place as you write about your life. You may help someone else to avoid them.

o   o   o

Here are two brief sketches of Christmas, one by my father, Jacob Funk, about a Christmas when he was a medic in the army in Russia, and one by me about my childhood Christmases. Do you see any similarity in what we remember?

Christmas, 1914

"Peace on earth, good will toward men," sang the angels that first Christmas Day. Yet on Christmas Eve, 1914, my country, Russia, was at war. Our unit had been stationed at Fort Dubno on the Eastern front when our officers received the command to move our train to a spur line until further orders arrived.

For a short while, time stood still that Christmas Eve as we waited for the morning. I pondered to myself. Where was I? What was I doing here?

I was in Red Cross train No. 195 S.Z. An old freight train had been hastily converted into a makeshift hospital on wheels. The twelve neatly made beds in each boxcar were still unoccupied, for we hadn't reached our destination—the war zone—as yet.

I was a volunteer medic, inexperienced and with little training. I knew, however, that when our train filled with wounded soldiers, I would be expected to do my part in nursing and comforting the men on the return trip to the hospitals in Kiev.

As we waited in our hospital train on the siding, tense yet eager to move on, we watched the military trains rush by us to the front. Train after train, car after car, loaded with bright young men, sped by us. Though they had everything to live for, they were being transported to the front to be slaughtered like cattle.

Some of these soldiers stared out the train windows at the passing scenery. A few waved to us, and we waved back. The movement was almost mechanical. Few men talked or cheered. Even in our train, the atmosphere was burdened by the silence among ourselves as we listened to the dull roar of the cannons in the distance.

Suddenly a passing train threw a bag of mail to us. Immediately our train became alive with noisy excitement as men from all cars gathered around the canvas bag. Letters. Parcels from home. We laughed. We cried. It was Christmas Eve. The mail reminded us of this fact once again.

As the letters and packages were opened, memories of warmth and love of family circles overwhelmed the men.

How great the longing to be at home to celebrate Christmas with loved ones!

A young soldier rushed out into the snowy night and brought back a scraggly little pine tree. He shoved it into a old boot to make it stand upright. We looked at the sad little unadorned Christmas tree, and again the tears flowed.

We ached to sing the old familiar carols, but we had been forbidden to use the German language, our mother tongue, because it was the language of the enemy. However, from a corner, the soft tones of a mouth organ playing *"Stille Nacht"* (Silent Night) brought quietness to our hearts. For a short while it seemed like "peace on earth."

Our peace was rudely shattered by a loud command to get ready to move. The Christmas tree was thrown out the door, the letters replaced in their envelopes, and the mouth organ silenced. The train rolled from its place on the siding to the main track toward the front.

I was apprehensive. What would we find there? How many wounded? How many dead? How many sweethearts, wives, and parents would never hear nor see their loved ones again?

When we reached the smoking, ravaged town of Brodi on the Austrian border, scenes of horror faced us on all sides. Few buildings had been left standing. People cowered for protection in cellars or craters created by bombs. An ancient cemetery had spewed up decaying coffins. Nearby we saw massive fresh graves carefully covered with pine tree branches. Buried underneath were the bodies of thousands of our brave young men.

But we had no time for fearing and wondering. Our work had begun. An endless stream of soldiers with haunted faces and ugly, gaping wounds waited their turn to be loaded onto our train. We worked steadily until every bed, every chair, and every corner of the train was full. Then the train started the return journey to the hospitals of Kiev. In our car the peace and quiet of a few hours ago now turned into screams and moans of pain.

The train stopped briefly at a little hamlet. Terrified faces peered into the open doors of the former freight cars. One old woman, face wrinkled and weary beneath her shawl, tugged at my sleeve. "Soldier, have you come from the front?" I nodded. Her hand grasped my arm more securely. "Did you see my son?" I looked down at the anxious eyes imploring me to say yes. How many times had she asked this question? How many more times would she ask it? Would she ever receive the answer she wanted to hear?

I lifted her hand gently from my arm as I sadly shook my head. I turned to answer the call of a sick soldier. I could not face her.

Christmas Day, 1914. For her, for the sick man, for me, there was yet no peace.

"They shall beat their swords into plowshares, and their spears into pruninghooks: nation shall not lift up sword against nation, neither shall they learn war any more," wrote the prophet Isaiah.

When will men learn? The answer is blowing in the wind.

Depression Christmas

Years ago, in northern Saskatchewan, when the frost had completely covered the windowpanes with furry ridges, we children would rub a spot clear with a forefinger until the bright, shining winter world again came

into view. Each child could view the outside through her
private peephole.

Today, when I rub the windowpane of memory, trying
to bring the depression years into focus, what I see first is
not a sparkly clean winter scene but a view of life that is
dingy with dust and despair.

It is summer, and I see Mother putting wet cloths
along the windowsills to keep the dirt out. I see Dad
counting relief vouchers instead of cash at the end of his
long day in his grocery store. I see the neighbor lady hoe-
ing long, meaningless hours in an unproductive garden,
and carrying pail after pail of water from the village well
to keep her few plants alive. I see my sisters and myself
pulling on our flour-sack underwear in the morning and
longing for something slithery and thin.

During the dirty thirties the passing freight trains dis-
charged scores of jobless hoboes into our community.
Old young men in worn clothing begged at our door for
a meal. The bench at the bank corner was crowded with
limp bodies barely holding up the empty faces, out of
which peered tired eyes. Through my mind flit memories
of a young boy caught stealing school lunches because he
was hungry, of a young friend crying in the cloakroom
because she was cold and her coat was too thin, of myself
longing to own a ten-cent box of crayons instead of only a
five-cent one at least once before I grew too old to enjoy
them.

A little brighter and clearer are the memories of the
small joys which highlighted those difficult years. The
rare gift of five cents bought a big bag of jelly beans, a
huge Sweet Marie bar, or a soft drink. Perhaps once or
twice a summer we tasted an ice-cream cone, licking
it carefully around the edge to preserve each precious drop.

We enjoyed many small pleasures which had no price, but which were priceless—wading in the dirty ditches after a summer rain, swishing the mud lazily through our toes; playing can-can with neighboring children on the empty lot; dangling our feet over the edge of the corral and watching the wild horses from the Alberta plains being broken; pulling hairs from their tails to make ourselves rings.

But then when winter came and snow blanketed the earth, despondency always changed to hope—at least in the hearts of the children for Christmas was coming. An aura of peace and goodwill encircled the struggling community for a little while and gave life a glory even the poor could enjoy. The village people moved closer to each other for spiritual warmth. Every depression child knew what Christmas was about, even though he or she didn't know the right words to talk about the incarnation. Christmas meant the return of joy and hope and love, even if only briefly. Without it, life would have been a perennial arid desert.

And so, the spot I have rubbed on memory's pane becomes suddenly very bright as I think of Christmas and the happy way it dominated our lives for several weeks. First came Eaton's mail-order catalog with its storehouse of wonders; then the carol singing in school and church, and the practicing for the annual programs. The Christmas agenda included the creation of gifts—out of more flour sacks, as well as papier-mâché, tin cans, and oilcloth. We children picked names in various gift exchanges. We endured Dad's teasing regarding the gift St. Nicholas might bring, even while we loved it. Mother baked several varieties of cookies—*Pfeffernüsse*, ammonia, oatmeal, and icebox—and stored them in the cold verandah. Some years she baked fruitcake. If we managed to eat twelve different kinds at twelve different homes, it meant twelve months of good luck for us.

I took my turn filling the bags of candy, nuts, and an orange for the children of the various rural schools which the school boards ordered from my dad's store. "Katie, come help fill another order." One-half pound of nuts, one-quarter pound of mixed candy, one Japanese orange. ..." Every child knew that no matter how slim parents' resources were, he or she would receive a bag of treats at school.

The depression years grow brightest in my mind as I think of the many times we, as a family, listened to Charles Dickens' "Christmas Carol" over the radio or of how we strung popcorn or painted walnut shells for tree decorations. The Christmas tree was decorated with real candles, which we lit once or twice a season under careful supervision of our elders.

Intermixed are memories of the Christmas concerts with their candid attempts to create joy with poems, plays, songs, and the coming of a real Santa Claus. We endured none of today's obvious attempts to manipulate children to speak an adult theological message which they don't understand. Christmas was joy, not piety. Costuming was important at these concerts, even if the costumes were only borrowed bathrobes for the wise men and shepherds, and cheesecloth and tarnished tinsel for the angels.

Occasionally we tasted a little ecumenicity by flocking to the Catholic church to see if their program was any better than ours or their candy bags any bigger.

And then, at last, came Christmas Day and the early morning rush to open the packages lying beside the bowls we had set out the night before. We were made of sterner stuff than those who reserve this event for Christmas Eve so they can sleep late the next day. We waited until the real day. We reveled in these gifts of love—unmerited, sometimes bought at great sacrifice, given for no other reason than this day was the celebration of Christ's birth.

And then, as swiftly as it had come, Christmas was over and we returned to our normal routine. Grownups wondered about next year's crop and worried about finding money to pay the bills. Children hoped that maybe this year there would be enough money for a storebought dress or a bicycle. Though the summer might again be dry and fruitless, the memory of Christmas joy eased the pressures and made life whole for a while. Each year after Christmas came spring and seedtime and hope. Maybe this year. . . .

CHAPTER TWO

How to Begin

Before you begin, be clear in your own mind what you are planning to write about those "dear dead days" which seem almost beyond recall. Your material will not be a work of fiction; the short story writer or novelist writes fiction, creating through the use of the imagination a piece of writing which may appear to have actually happened. Sometimes fiction may seem more real than real life, but in actuality it is an imaginative version of life as it might be.

Nor will your writing be a history book, although it will probably include some historical material. A historian records significant events affecting a nation or an institution, usually explaining their causes.

Nor is your work a biography, which is the account of the life story of another person. You will be moving into the area of autobiography. Some scholars see a clear distinction between autobiography and memoirs; others think the dividing line is too fine to make a difference. As a biographer reflects the life of another person in writing, showing us a faithful picture of that human being on his

way through life, so you, in your memoirs, will try to give
a faithful picture of your experiences and how they affected you. Both biography and autobiography teach the
art of living directly. You are saying to your reader, "This
is the way it worked (or didn't work) for me."

An autobiography is usually considered as a more con-
trolled form of writing than memoir writing. Some
writers consider an autobiography a work of art in which
form and content are welded together by the writer into
a unified whole. In writing your memoirs, you will
probably be more concerned with subject matter than
with form. You will not be as concerned with the completeness of the picture you are presenting of your life, as
with the completeness of each of a series of portraits of
your life which reveal your sureties and confusions, your
movement ahead and the times you had to step back. In
calling your writing memoirs, you are already telling
your audience you are selecting, emphasizing, and inter-
preting the events of your life. You do not profess to be a
professional writer, but you have something you wish to
say through these recollections and reminiscences about
how you felt the quality of your life to be.

Biography, autobiography, and memoirs are usually
interesting and entertaining to read, because they move
close to the real person. They also encourage and inspire.
They may show how important genetic factors were in
the lives of some persons who followed in the vocational
footsteps of their parents, and also how unimportant such
factors were in the lives of others who chose their own
pathway. Memoirs frequently reveal how individuals discovered the world, and what they did with those bits of
discovery to come to a sense of life's calling. Yet memoirs
should not dwell only on public successes and major

crises. Private bits of knowledge should also be included to round out the picture.

So, before you begin, keep in mind that memoir writing is for anyone, not only for important persons. You don't need to take writing courses before you begin. You don't need to be a publishing writer. The important thing is to be yourself. Write honestly about your way of remembering and seeing life instead of looking for the words and experiences which you think your readers may expect to find in your writing. Once you get started, you will find yourself walking an enjoyable path of companionship with the person you used to be, as you find out more about that individual.

Before You Take Pen in Hand

At first you will find yourself excited and eager to get started. That's good. Hang onto that feeling. You'll need it when the going gets rough. But here's my first bit of advice: Don't try to write the whole thing at one sitting. Begin small. Very small. Start with a small goal—writing down one small memory.

The task of writing your memoirs may be harder work than you visualize it to be. Chopping wood all day is hard on body muscles; writing is hard on the brain. Thinking forces you to stretch your mind, and at times you may get weary of brain-work and even downright annoyed that you can't remember something you think should be near the surface.

So make the task of writing fun. Look upon it as good times with old times. Perhaps even a ministry of love. You are planning to give part of yourself as a gift to your readers. Take time to think yourself into the project, and don't become too concerned when you find that some days you spend more time thinking than writing. Professional writers find that to be true also.

One of your main sources of information will probably be your own memory (unless you kept a journal), and memory can be as evasive as a mouse behind the couch. Memory may also be faulty. It has a mysterious way of preserving some experiences in their entirety, down to the cherry which always topped the whipped cream on Mother's piece of apple pie, and blanking others out completely. Time also has a strange way of changing the color of an experience or even transferring it into a different time period; it may even get rid of some of the people you know were present.

Most of us can remember only vaguely. We have to strain to recall the past, so plan to use as many techniques as possible to stir your memory. Dig for the experience you want to put into words.

At first, as you coax and prod your memory, you will remember only a bare outline of an event and a few skimpy details. I have many such skeleton memories. I can recall one evening when I was quite young, about four or five, when a fire swept through one whole block of our small community in late spring, taking with it a bowling alley, a restaurant, three general stores, a drugstore, and a doctor's office. I recall seeing dirty, melting snow. I see Mother standing by the window looking anxiously at the flurry of activity at the end of the block. By her stands the big wicker baby buggy with my baby sister sleeping in it. She was born in April, so this event must have happened when she was an infant.

Two other details come to mind: (1) Father rushes home to get the canvas used to protect our car against the weather. He plans to cover the roof of our store with it and then wet the tarp to keep the flying sparks from igniting the shingles. (2) Green sleighs drawn by patient horses stand on the road in front of the burning buildings. Dad said later there had been considerable looting, because most of the local residents, busy battling the fire, could not guard the wares dragged into the streets.

What can I do with these scattered bits of material? At some point, when you reach a similar impasse, you may be tempted to give up and put your pen back in the drawer. Memory is too weak to put together the shattered pieces of the events of such a night, or others like it. Yet if I leave out this incident, I may leave out an important link in my story, one which explains my present fear of fires. So what can you do when you come to a similar problem?

When you begin writing your memoirs, it's like starting a cooking or woodworking project. First, you have to gather your materials to see what you have on hand and what you need. Here are some things to look for:

1. Write up all incidents you remember well. Don't worry about style, punctuation, and spelling at this time. Don't let such insignificant matters scare you off. Put energy into your pen or typewriter and keep writing. Purchase a loose-leaf notebook or folder so that, as you work, you can sort and file as you move along.

2. Make a family tree, or as much of a family tree as you are able to recall at this point. Because you are writing a book of memoirs and not a genealogy, don't be too concerned about getting all the dates accurately; but you will find it helpful to display the tree before you as you write to keep family relationships clear. Add dates of births, deaths, and marriages if you can.

3. Read other memoirs, history books, novels, and

short stories, that took place during the period you are
writing about. Many books are available about the depression, World War II, or pioneering days in America. If
you plan to include much about the silent fifties and tur-
bulent sixties, look for books in your local library which
discuss national events in society during these periods.
Such general reading will help you put your own story
into a broader perspective.

4. As you have time and energy, read old copies of
church and community newspapers, available in historical libraries. As you browse through old newspapers
you find your memory jogged again and again when you
come upon some fact which matches your experience.
Write these little details down, so you can add them to
your own story; but use your own words to do so. Locate
old mail-order catalogs, phone directories, almanacs, and
other kinds of magazines of the period in which you are
interested. I found out from some old clippings which
business establishments had been burned.

5. Take time to wander through old museums and
cemeteries. A history of a community is often engraved
on the tombstones of those who lie buried there. We
have an "orphans' graveyard" near the community
where I live. When my children were younger, we used
to go on discovery tours in this graveyard. We learned
that under the mulberry bushes and spruce trees are
buried some "fresh-air orphans" sent to a church or-
phanage from Chicago about the turn of the century.
They came to Kansas to give them a better environment
in which to grow up. A number died of the diseases
which plagued children in the years before vaccinations,
such as scarlet fever and diphtheria.

6. Look for old letters, photo albums, diaries, college

yearbooks, newspaper clippings, budget books, and other family writings. Each may yield a bit of information you can use. Talk to other members of the family and let them pick your brain as you question them.

7. A good way to transplant yourself into the past is to draw a diagram of the floor plan of the house in which you lived as a child. You could also draw a plan of the farmyard, the schoolhouse, the church, and perhaps even the town in which you grew up. Add doors, windows, and furniture to your floor plan. You will find that a house that seemed very large to you as a child now won't accommodate the furniture you know was in it. When you have completed these details, alongside the diagram make a list of events that happened at a particular period of your life. Add lists of people who were part of your life. Keep prodding your memory to bring back some of these events. This process is called brainstorming and is an important part of any writing project. Let the lists grow. At this point make no judgments about what to include or exclude, what to emphasize or skim over, in your final draft.

Make these lists by groups or categories:

Home:

> One Christmas we all got the measles and had to stay home all vacation.
>
> Our playhouse became a flying machine. We argued always about who would handle the controls (nails hammered into a piece of wood). The machine made trips to many distant lands and sometimes dared to land.

School:

> One year I was the fairy in the school

play, for I was the teacher's pet, and the other children didn't like it.

We used to play on the fire escape.

In grade one we held teas for our mothers.

The high school boys sometimes got drunk at parties.

When no one was watching us, we cooked fudge in the lab.

Church:

We children sat outside and talked whenever the grownups had a serious meeting we couldn't attend. Sometimes we played hide-and-go-seek.

Each Sunday we had to read a verse from the lesson in German. I hated doing this because I couldn't read German well. One Sunday the teacher was kind and told me I could read it in English.

Every Sunday we got a nickel to put into the offering. I always wished for a quarter like my friend received from her father.

Revival meetings were scary things to go to. I never knew for sure what to do.

The Empty Lot:

We played Run, My Good Sheep, Run for hours until Mother called us in.

In the evenings we lay on the prickly grass and watched the northern lights dart across the sky, or we told ghost stories and scared ourselves so much we didn't want to go home in the dark.

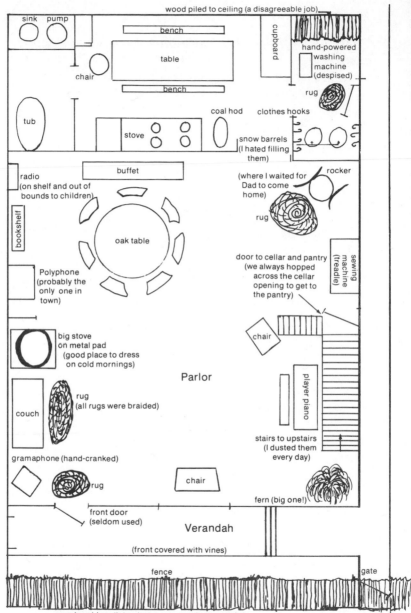

wood piled to ceiling (a disagreeable job)

sink   pump

bench

cupboard

table

hand-powered washing machine (despised)

chair

rug

tub

stove

coal hod   clothes hooks

snow barrels (I hated filling them)

radio (on shelf and out of bounds to children)

buffet

(where I waited for Dad to come home)

rocker

rug

bookshelf

oak table

Polyphone (probably the only one in town)

door to cellar and pantry (we always hopped across the cellar opening to get to the pantry)

sewing machine (treadle)

chair

big stove on metal pad (good place to dress on cold mornings)

Parlor

couch

rug (all rugs were braided)

player piano

gramaphone (hand-cranked)

rug

chair

stairs to upstairs (I dusted them every day)

fern (big one!)

front door (seldom used)

Verandah

(front covered with vines)

fence

gate

wooden sidewalk (we lost our money in the cracks)

Continue with such lists, including the community or a friend's home.

Another way of beginning is to ask yourself why you remember some of these events. Usually you will find that some strong emotion accompanied them, such as pride, joy, shame, regret, bewilderment. So you could make lists of times you felt very happy or times that brought sadness into your life:

> I went to a funeral with my father and sister. I was sure the woman in the coffin was my mother. Her hair was red like Mother's. I rushed home to see if Mother was still alive.

> I used to wonder why the old men of the town liked to sit in front of my father's store by the hour, doing nothing but eating sunflower seeds and talking. Now I think I know.

> I wondered why we never had store-bought clothes when they looked so nice.

> I wondered whether I would ever get to the place where I wouldn't have to pile wood, dry dishes, wash floors, hang up clothes, hoe the garden, and bring in snow to melt for water.

> I often wished we could eat store-bought bread with butter *and* jam. We ate our bread with only one spread.

8. Another similar approach is to make a time line of your life, similar to the chart on pages 49 and 50. At one end put down the date of your birth and at the other the present date. Now, at the appropriate points, locate the "firsts" and the main events of your life, such as the first Christmas you can remember, first illness, first school day, first love, first kiss, first job, first failure, first time

you openly took a stand for some position, your marriage, births of children, deaths in the family that affected you, first spiritual awakening, first public speech, first long travel, and so forth. On the other side of the line add events which were taking place in the world beyond your own, but which affected yours, such as developments in the fields of communication, transportation, philosophy, politics, religion, science, climate, terrain, health care, and the like. You can get some of these events from history books. What you are doing is putting your life into a context of world events and establishing the socioeconomic and sociopolitical background in which you grew up. As you do this, you will find still other memories coming to you to connect with these changes in the world beyond yours.

As you begin gathering materials, ask questions, and don't hesitate to let others read what you write. It may be a little frightening at first, but well worthwhile. Discussion is like a butter churn; it helps ideas to separate and formulate, so talk to children, brothers, and sisters. In the conversation new memories will spring forth like mushrooms after a rain. One casual recollection may draw forth a host of others. Collect the scattered experiences of childhood in this way, even if you won't use them all later on.

Don't worry that you're not doing much writing just yet. That will come. Spend a little time each week with your project, so it remains a constant companion. Don't get discouraged. Writing is usually 90 percent perspiration and 10 percent inspiration. It will probably be the same for you. But enjoy the new challenge it brings to you.

Perhaps you're beginning to think of what visible form

World War I
Russian Revolution

	1923	Parents arrive in Canada
Gas lights		My birth in Saskatchewan
Horses		
		First family car
Epidemics		Move to Blaine Lake
		Big fire in Blaine Lake
	1930	Enter grade one
Depression		
Drought		First radio
Dust		First camping experience
Grasshoppers		
Town wells		Visit of King and Queen
Dirt roads		to Saskatoon
Electricity		See first airplane close up
		I begin high school
World War II		Schoolmates enlist in army
	1940	
Iceboxes		First love
		High school graduation
Gravel roads		
		First job (legal secretary)
Booming economy		Baptism
		Attend Bible college
		Marriage
		Birth of Joanna
	1950	
		First refrigerator
Paved roads		
		Birth of Susan
		First home telephone

		Birth of Christine
Vietnam War		Illness of husband
		Birth of James
	1960	
		First article published
Race riots		Death of husband
Civil rights		First driver's license
Hippies		Return to working world
Jesus people		First television set
Church renewal		Purchase of present home
movements		First child leaves home
		B.A. degree
		Second child leaves home
	1970	
		First air-conditioner
Richard Nixon		First major illness
Watergate		Susan marries Roger
Jerry Ford		M.A. degree
Jimmy Carter		First airplane ride
Inflation		Third child leaves home
		First grandchild
		First books published
		First overseas travel.

this gift of yours can take. We'll discuss that in the next chapter, but to give you a little preview, here's something one of my daughters did one Christmas. Christine gave the other members of the family the story, in simple typewritten form embellished with a few line drawings, of a serious illness she experienced. I cherish her gift more than an electric knife or a pair of kidskin gloves because she trusted us with the record of her feelings during a difficult time of her life.

The Caging of Chris, by Chris Wiebe
I give this book to The Wiebe family with a smile.

Inky blackness washed over me, forcing me to clutch the bathroom door. As my knees sank to the floor, I cried out—

"Mother! Mother—I need help. ...."

Immediately I heard her footsteps in the darkness. Then I felt her arms, lifting and dragging me as I stumbled back to bed.

Mother's voice came from a great distance. "Can you help pull yourself on the bed?" she asked. "I simply can't lift you that far." I woke up completely and realized I had blacked out again. With my last ounce of energy, I hoisted first my trunk and then each leg, resting after each effort.

Mother had struggled alone enough with my illness. The next morning we went to the hospital to let someone else battle against the lupus inside me. The following incidents trace my struggle to climb out of a major attack of this disease, beginning with my stay in the hospital.

o   o   o

It must have been my third night in the hospital. I turned myself over and back, over and back—like bun dough in Mother's hands. At about 12:30, a large white figure appeared in the room to ask a rather obvious question—"You're *still* awake?"

As unsuspecting as the expanding dough before the final punchdown, I explained my frustrations of the past two hours to the nurse. She mumbled something like, "We'll fix that!" which should have warned me for what followed.

It didn't. The knife-like shot left me a deflated mass of

self-pity. I felt so limp, so angry—and a lot smarter. "The next time that nurse checks on me," I decided, "she'll find me relaxed and sleeping like a baby—whether or not I am!"

*   *   *

Gray light filtered through the venetian blinds onto a cart of flowers in all stages of decay. The nurse apologized for waking me at six o'clock and left the room.

I fought to reach the water glass, my swollen wrists and elbows fighting back. Success came after several attempts, and the water washed away the alcohol taste left by the thermometer and eased the burning in my stomach.

Now there was nothing to do but wait. And wait. And wait. I thought about how long I had been lying in this bed. The two and a half weeks seemed more like two and a half months. My fists dug into the sheets, as if to push me far away from the bed, the room, the hospital.

Maybe today he would let me go home! The thought prompted a cautious smile. I decided not to say anything about it to the doctor, but let him surprise me instead.

Breakfast finally appeared and I tried to chew the cold, hard toast. When nausea interrupted my eating I thought, "I would get better faster if I could eat Mother's homemade buns."

I closed my eyes, but the noise of people, carts, and machines prevented me from sleeping. Remembering the agonized shouting during the night of the cancer patient across the hall, I thought, "It would be easier to sleep at home."

At last the doctor's voice drifted to me from a room

nearby. Three minutes stretched into five, ten, fifteen—and there he was, smiling, questioning, pushing, and listening. I held my breath, the hope straining inside of me. The doctor gathered his instruments, turned, and smiled. Yellow sunlight flashed on the stethoscope at his neck as he disappeared around the door, already thinking of the next patient. For a moment I stared at the empty doorway. Quietly, bitterly—I wept.

o   o   o

Three times, I repinned the button to my thin cotton nightgown. After a business-like yank had straightened the wayward sheets, I attacked the jigsaw puzzle of the baby in the bathtub.

Just as I found the eye of the rubber duck, the doctor marched in. Hastily I snapped it in place and pushed the puzzle aside.

He turned away, studying the charts on the dresser and the nurses' reports on his clipboard. Without a word, he approached the bed to poke and probe and listen. After all the instruments were assembled again, he advanced to the end of the bed, turned—and saw the immaculate sheets; the peach nightgown (two sizes too big); and the little button. His head snapped forward to read the brief message: "Bloom where you are planted."

For a moment he beamed at me, his eyes dancing about. Then slyly he gave my toe a roguish pull, and sauntered out the door.

o   o   o

(There are numerous advantages in living in a hospital for three weeks—presents for one. One sister made a mobile for me that slowly revolved, flashing absurd glimpses of ten grinning, staring, laughing faces. Another sister presented a smock, and my brother brought an oval stone, sanded and smoothed to almost perfect symmetry on the beach where he had found it. But by far the most significant gift was Mother's Homemade Buns.)

Day after day, the stage was set before me. The first act came and went—usually some pureed delicacy— followed by grape Jello, and finally the ice cream. Meal after meal this succession of liquid delights disappeared down my throat—for about ten minutes. Invariably my stomach staged a curtain call of the entire cast of characters.

After a week of such entertainment I was growing bored with both my stomach and the hospital food. Finally I asked Mother if she would bring me some *real* food. I suggested borscht (vegetable beef soup), *Vereneke* (cottage cheese dumplings), or apple pie. I settled for Mother's Homemade Buns.

The day these culinary wonders arrived, almost a crowd had gathered in my room. I rocked one gently in my hands, breathing in great whiffs of Mother and Saturday morning baking. I spread and respread the butter and jelly. Finally I sank my teeth into the bun—and everyone laughed. Ignoring them all, I finished the bun and stored the rest in a drawer. "That way," I thought, "if I'm ever faced with rubber toast again I'll simply have a bun instead."

o   o   o

Finally the morning arrived when the doctor said, "You can go home as soon as your mother can come to get you."

For ten seconds after he left I stared at the ceiling and

gloated. I couldn't wait any longer to call the nurse. At last she arrived and I told her the good news.

"Would you help me walk to the telephone so I can phone my mother?" I asked. My fingers fumbled at dialing the telephone for the first time in three weeks.

"Hello, Mother? This is Chris! The doctor says I can go home as soon as you come, so can you come soon?"

"*Well*. We'll come get you right away," she said.

I put down the receiver and let out a sigh. My stay in the hospital was almost over. Shakily I walked back to my room and sank onto the bed.

When Mother arrived I was still lying there, hugging myself and smiling at everything. I couldn't lie down while Mother and James were collecting my things; I had to sit up and watch, even though I couldn't help.

I put on my housecoat and wool slippers and eased into the wheelchair waiting by my bed. Away we flew—down the hallway, past the nurses' desk, and out into the summer morning.

o   o   o

(Through with the hospital! So I thought. But the hospital was not finished with me. About two months after my first visit, the doctor discovered a defect in my anatomy that required a simple operation. The following incident explains some of my feelings while under anesthesia.)

At 11:00 that morning a nurse came into my room and gave me a shot—to relax me before the operation, she explained. Thirty minutes later, when a cart was wheeled in that would take me to the operating room, I was completely relaxed. As I rolled onto the cart, I felt as if I was tumbling over and over and over. . . .

Slowly, ceiling after ceiling disappeared behind me till we reached the operating room. From somewhere I heard a man singing to himself. Then a shower-capped nurse put a needle in my wrist and I lost consciousness rapidly.

Somewhere in the haze I remember asking a question that frightened me: Who is Christine Wiebe? I was an utter stranger to myself. My friends and family were far away and I was lost in a haze of color and lights and strange people.

I woke up to see three sets of one nurse pulsating rapidly above me. Her voice sounded far away as she told me the operation was all over. I tried to tell her I had no pain, but my words came out thickly and slowly. I wondered if she understood me.

Some time later I found myself back in my own room and I waved in the general direction of my roommate—my eyes were not focusing yet, but I could distinguish a blur that waved back.

As I gradually began to feel like myself again, I noticed a bottle hung upside down above me with tiny bubbles steadily rising to the surface. My eyes followed the clear plastic tube from the bottle to a needle taped around my wrist.

Nurses came and went; the bottle disappeared; and I swallowed some orange juice that promptly reappeared. Soon after the doctor dropped by to tell me I could go home, I fell asleep.

At last—I heard Mother's footsteps far down the hall. Closer and closer came the quick staccato tap-tap-tap. And then the warmth of her arms was around me and I could see the concern and love in her eyes.

For several weeks after I left the hospital, I spent much of the day in bed. Each morning I gingerly pushed my feet out of my cocoon and shuffled over to the window. A yank on the curtains released a flood of sunshine, bathing my room with the new day. Then I gazed for a moment across the vacant football field to a tiny pasture surrounded on three sides with trees and barns and houses, so I saw only a corner of the cemetery behind it.

One morning I flung back the covers and rushed to open the curtains—to be caught in the spell of the sun rising through clouds of mist that rose and parted and fell, obscuring everything beyond the pasture. One silent tree stood half-shrouded by itself, till without warning a sleek brown horse pranced up to the fence, whipping the mist with its tail and whispering in the leaves of the tree branches.

CHAPTER THREE

Giving It Form

Anytime you make something, you have to decide what form it will take. If you bake a cake, you have to decide whether to bake it in an oblong, round, or square pan. If you build a house, you have to decide whether it will be ranch-style, two-story, or perhaps even a geodesic dome. Then, after making the plan, each stroke of the saw and each blow of the hammer requires new decisions.

After you have collected some materials for your memoirs and before you launch into full-scale writing, you will also have to decide what form your writing will take. If you just let the words flow onto the paper, like spilled milk, they may drip off the edge and disappear. Often, as you read other people's writing, you may not be aware that the writer had a form in mind as he or she wrote. Most news stories are written in what is called the inverted pyramid form, with a lead which summarizes the main ideas in the article, and then a series of paragraphs, each of which includes the facts of the news story in descending order of importance. Poems can take many forms, including sonnets, odes, couplets, blank verse, and free verse. Even articles and short stories have some form or framework which holds together the superstructure the writers build on it.

This book has a framework which I worked out before I began writing, but after I had collected the material. Your memoirs will stand the test of time better if you consciously consider some form. You can decide this matter now or when you have sorted and arranged the material you have gathered. Basic to form is to answer the question: What do I want my writing to do for the reader? What do I want to convey?

One of the most common forms, although not necessarily the best one, is the development of your memoirs in *chronological order*. In this type of linear writing, you begin with your early childhood, perhaps even the lives of your parents, and move through each life period to retirement, or wherever you may be when you complete the work. If you choose chronological order, you should be aware of several problems you may encounter. Persons who deliberately choose this form often had the achieving of a successful career as one of life's main goals, and they propose to show the path they traveled to that goal, from beginning to end.

Unless you have some similar reason for choosing this method of telling your story, you may have to work your way through a great deal of dull and uninteresting material before you get to the real reasons why you started writing your memoirs. You may also be tempted at times to skip big sections of your life, because you can't remember what happened or you don't think they are necessary to the telling. At other times, you may find yourself moving very slowly over other parts because you have more material on them, and yet they may not be as significant to your story as the parts you skip over lightly. This hop, skip, and jump method may annoy the reader because he or she has to figure out what happened in the left-out sections. Yet the chronological form is probably the easiest and most frequently used. Don't dismiss it too quickly.

A second type of memoirs uses *thematic development* to deal with the experiences of life. If you choose this treatment, select one or more basic themes (fundamental features of human life) and develop them, bringing in biographical material as it fits. However, do not feel compelled to tell every detail of your life story. You might consider such themes as vocational growth, life in the family, spiritual truths, life values, political views, nature, love, death, travel experiences, relationships with friends and family, school days, and so forth. In *Surprised by Joy*, C. S. Lewis picks the theme of his conversion to Christianity and includes enough of his background to explain his decision to become a follower of Christ. For more information about his biography, a reader has to turn to other books. In my book *Alone: A Widow's Search for Joy* (Tyndale House Publishers), I deal primarily with the topic of widowhood and leave out other aspects of my life which do not fit this subject. This combination of chronological and thematic treatment, selecting only certain periods of your life to reveal some important truths you have learned or experiences you have enjoyed, is worth considering.

You may also choose to write *sketches* from your life, loosely tied together, which get meaning from their emphasis on private moments and private feelings. These might be arranged like photographs in an album, according to chronology or according to some theme. They may be serious or humorous. You are simply offering the reader a series of reminiscences to enjoy with you.

You may want to use *journals* and *letters*, or both, to record your life story, if you have been in the habit of keeping journal writings or carbon copies of letters. You will find diaries useful for establishing facts and accounts of day-to-day happenings, but not as valuable as journal entries for providing substance for your writing. A journal is a record of your intellectual and emotional or spiritual life—your thought life. It includes a record of the event and your reactions to it and conveys a picture of your inner person at various times of life. Although diaries are helpful in providing the exact dates when something happened, their bare-bones approach is not usually interesting to the reader. The danger in using either journals or diaries too much is that you may overburden your memoirs with unnecessary detail, which slows the reader to a monotonous crawl.

Who Is Your Audience?

Pick an audience to write for, perhaps a grandchild or a friend. As you write keep that person or persons in mind and respond to their questions and needs. Is your reader a friend or stranger? Write as if you are carrying on a dialogue with that person sitting across the table from you. With professional writers, that audience is usually firmly fixed in their minds and helps them communicate on a consistent level. The audience you select will help you decide several matters: choice of language, choice of subject, tone, amount of detail in describing events, how much you will reveal about yourself, and your judgments about yourself and your friends.

The choice of audience will also help you decide what slant or frame of reference you will adopt as you write. In "The Nose," a short story by the Russian writer Gogol, one of the characters, a barber, begins his day with a breakfast of bread, onions, and salt. "Bread, onions, and salt?" asked one of my literature students. "Who eats such a breakfast?" I explained that during the depression I could remember people putting just about anything between two slices of bread to give the sandwich flavor. Radishes, cucumbers, or tomatoes were commonly used; meat sandwiches were rare. Bread and onions sounded possible to me.

The student was reading the nineteenth-century story from his perspective of the twentieth century: onions and bread need a hamburger between them. He and Gogol were working from two frames of reference. I'm reminded of the diner in the restaurant who ordered coffee and doughnuts. When he found he couldn't eat all he had ordered, he asked if anyone wanted his extra doughnut. No one did. So he wrapped it in a napkin and took it with him. One of the diners still eating commented that the man must have grown up during the depression. Everyone in the diner was below the age of thirty. They probably couldn't understand his concern at letting a doughnut go to waste; he probably couldn't understand why no one jumped at his offer of free food.

As you write, remember that you have been molded by the values your family and community considered essential for successful living. You probably accepted new ideas only if you could fit them into your frame of reference. I've had to change my views about various matters from time to time. Before my husband died, I thought babysitting was an evil habit no good mother supported. I battled much guilt when I had to take my youngest child to a babysitter every day, all day, while I worked to support the family. Eventually I had to change my frame of reference to make room for mothers to work outside the home without guilt.

You don't need to apologize for your frame of reference, but simply recognize it is there. If you were once a political conservative and now have more liberal views don't hesitate to say so—nor need you be embarrassed by the position you once held. These are facts of life. Occasionally you will have to include extra information for the person who reads your memoirs with a different frame of reference—your grandchild, for example, who was brought up in an affluent age with electricity, jet planes, processed foods, and central heating. He may not understand what you mean when you write about handcranked engines and iceboxes—or even privies!

New writers sometimes have difficulty with the point of view or the particular perspective from which the story is written. As you write, remember that the real person behind each story is you. So write from the point of view of "I" and not "we" or even "the writer." Make it your own story all the way through. If you use the "we" point of view, you appear to speak for all members of your family or class, as if you know all and see all. When you write about a group experience, instead of saying, "We all felt happy about the announcement," ask yourself whether you know for a fact that this statement was true. Perhaps someone didn't feel the same as you did. Change it to read: "I felt happy about the announcement. As I looked at my friends, I saw big smiles on their faces as the teacher read us the details." Now you are reporting a true fact.

You can write honestly only what you saw and heard and smelled and felt and thought yourself. You do not know what others thought unless they told you, but you can record what expressions you saw on their faces, or what they did when they looked happy or sad.

The point of view in memoirs is always your own, because these memoirs are yours and not your friend's. Don't let the reader lose sight of you out of a false sense of modesty. You are the main character in your story. You must assume your readers will be interested in what you say primarily because the story concerns you; the readers want the details about that person who is emerging from the pages as a living individual. The important thing is to write in such a way that no one but you could step into the shoes of the person being written about. Claim what is uniquely your own by writing your story—not your sister's or brother's.

You have a responsibility to convey information clearly and accurately, unless, of course, you want your story to be viewed as fiction. Be as precise as possible, especially regarding dates, numbers, place names, and so forth. But even with the goal of accuracy, you will find the temptation slips in to write about your experience in the way everyone expects it to be said, and to use the terminology which everyone uses, especially high-sounding words and phrases. Here are two examples of writing about the feelings of an immigrant in a new country. Which one was written to impress? Which one did you enjoy reading? Which one will you remember well enough to tell someone else what it said about beginning life anew?

Free at Last
Free at last, thank God Almighty, I'm free at last! I feel

like a slave to whom liberation has been granted. But when the liberty bell tolls in this new land it also introduces new responsibilities never considered before. Leaving behind relatives and friends, and the way of life I inherited, in another country is not all wine and roses. The wine ferments, and thorns encircle the roses. But I will become accustomed to the falls, learn new ways of picking myself up; and independence in this new land will become a proud possession I will protect till the day I am free from the bonds of this world forever.

The thought of that kind of independence inspires me to be a motivated citizen, willing and eager to begin my work here. With innumerable dreams to fulfill and aspirations to ponder, I dare not brake the enthusiasm billowing within my soul lest I be left behind in a cloud of dust never again to regain the motivation to succeed that is as essential to my new life as fuel is to an automobile. I'm sure I have such motivation, but I pray I may be motivated to accomplish something in this new country, whether it is economically, spiritually, socially, or a combination of all three.

A Clean Tablecloth and White Curtains

My parents migrated to Canada from Russia in 1923. The trip was long and tiring, especially with an infant and a toddler. They traveled with fear as their silent companion for much of the way, for who knew at what checkpoint the officials might say, "Your papers aren't in order," or "Your health isn't good enough." But the journey ended without incident. Now they were finally in Saskatchewan among relatives who welcomed them heartily.

That first night, a Saturday, was spent at the Schellenbergs' home, which was simply furnished, but clean and attractive. Mrs. Schellenberg, wearing a clean white apron, set the table for the evening meal, spreading it first with a smooth white tablecloth. Mother recalls how she watched these preparations and wondered whether the day would ever come when she could serve guests from a white tablecloth while wearing a white apron. What she and Dad owned at that point was limited. A *samovar* (Russian tea urn), a few dishes, some clothes and bedding, and a half-dozen blue polka-dotted diapers for my baby sister Annie. These had been quickly sewn before leaving Russia—out of the only available material. Dad had 25 cents in his pocket. The rest of the $10 saved for the trip had been spent in London, England, where Dad had bought a few essential items for the children and a jumper for Mother, so she would have at least one presentable garment.

Their hosts showed Mother and Dad around the house, including the playhouse for their children, in the brief tour. Mother marveled that the windows of the playhouse were draped with clean white curtains. *Will I ever have curtains like that in my home?* Mother dared to hope.

After supper, Mr. Schellenberg offered Dad a job clerking in one of his stores, to begin Monday morning. Dad accepted eagerly. Clerking was his vocation. He liked business. Twenty-five cents wouldn't buy much in terms of curtains, aprons, and tablecloths, but it represented hope for a better life. Both of my parents assure me that from that moment they never again looked back to Russia. They had chosen to live in Canada where there was possibility of fathers working instead of going to war, and of mothers cooking with real food instead of grain husks, and of children playing in playhouses instead of huddling in bedclothes all day because of the cold. Twenty-five cents was enough to begin this new life.

Write about what you know. Obviously you are an expert on your own life. Your past experiences do not have to be dramatic to write about them. Most people have about as much experience as they can handle, even if they never traveled more than fifty miles from the house where they were born. The observant person can see the deeper meaning behind each small event, whether it is weeding the garden for the tenth time or watching the sparrows nesting in the crosspiece of the clothesline. Read the story at the end of this chapter, by my daughter Joanna, in which she picks apart a small insignificant event in her childhood. Be willing to tell your experiences as they were. Share yourself with the reader at the *feeling* as well as the *fact* level to establish a common bond between you. Though you are writing about a time when you went courting in a horse and buggy for people dashing about on motorcycles and in sports cars, the feelings of hope, joy, discouragement, and failure never change. The way of life is like a road or path. Any path has its limits or edges where the bushes and rocks hinder walking. In your memoirs you are describing the road you traveled and also the limits or edges of that road. Sometimes it was too narrow and you felt pinched for room. At other times it became too broad and you got lost. Admit these upsetting experiences and disturbing memories. They add tension and interest to your writing. Food cooked without salt is tasteless. Food with too much sugar is too sweet to swallow. Season your writing with both sugar and salt.

In this writing you have the wonderful opportunity to take a peek over your own shoulder at yourself as a young person, and to watch that person from the new viewpoint of added years and experience. You will meet the child you once were moving back through the maze of memories to greet you. You will recall what that child or young person dreamed, hoped, and accomplished. At times you may find yourself struggling with contradictions and ambiguities in your own sense of identity as you work your way through these memories. Who is writing these memoirs? Is it the person you are now, or is it that youngster who caught tadpoles in the pond and skipped rope on the sidewalk every evening? Is it the hard-working farmer you were for forty or more years, or the husband and father who enjoyed family life? Is it a minister's wife, comfortable in her role, or a woman who longed for freedom to move in new directions?

This feeling of ambiguity of identity is not unusual. As you let yourself into the past, you may find yourself moving deeply within yourself in a voyage of self-discovery, and you may learn you have even more to give your reader than you had first planned.

A Ten-Cent Bar of Toffee

My father was an underpaid minister to a small and devout church on the dry prairies of Saskatchewan. Our family was not given to indulgences, but I do recall one summer, when I was in the fourth grade, we packed our 1953 brown Chevy and traveled north.

We left the land of plains and decrepit farms, and entered a new country. Waves of hills undulated to the horizon. These swellings of the earth were richly napped with grey-green grasses, gold-tipped in the evening sunlight. Springing from the hills were mats of bushes, weighted with ripening fruits: gooseberries, chokecherries, saskatoon berries. Spread palely over the mounds of the earth were patches of wild roses, pink and white and flowering sparsely in the thin soil. Miles from the car, the ragged arms of a tree embraced a curve of the earth. Swirling streams of dust eddied behind the car, settling softly.

Ahead, the road stretched soundlessly as it slid between the swells. The car probed past the hills to a place of jagged rocks, green and profuse bush, and small lakes. No one lived here, I thought. Yet, Father drove further and further north until we stopped where the road ended, on the shores of a blue lake, ringed by evergreens. Here five or six cabins lined the rocky beach. We rented one for five dollars. Here we fished and swam and lived a totally free life for six glorious days.

We had to go home again, of course. I sat quietly in the back seat of the car, sucking on a large slab of yellow MacIntosh's toffee, working it into a ball in my mouth, stretching it out until it was white, rolling it into a ball again, licking it and licking it.

In the middle of the general wilderness we saw a worn-out farm. The barn had lost its roof; the cows were as thin as slats in a board fence; a few crazed roosters scratched in the dusty yard. A quiet man of about forty came to meet our car, willing to talk, bringing with him his young daughter. He told us about the hail that had torn a huge hole in the kitchen roof. And the crops that didn't grow.

"Would you like to move south?" Father asked him, a charitable impulse no doubt moving in his heart.

"No," he replied. He liked it here. They were alone. They could live to themselves.

The little girl gazed at me: a fat contented child, sucking on a ten-cent piece of toffee. I felt vaguely embarrassed and wished that we would leave this place.

"Joanna," Father said later, as we sped down the road, dusting the fields, "why did you keep your candy to yourself? Why didn't you share it with that little girl?" Suddenly I was overcome with a deep sense of shame. She probably didn't even know what toffee was. I didn't really need it, did I? But it was too late.

This was my first major lesson in living, and I suppose I could draw a lot of morals from it. "Share." "Don't associate with those beneath you because it will only make them jealous." "No matter how poor you are, there's always someone poorer." But let's leave the production of morals.

I have always carried with me a mental image of that girl. She was a skinny child, wearing nothing but a cotton dress. She had gazed at me as though I were a little rich girl (something new to me!), with wonder, and perhaps even resentment in her eyes.

When I was home again I felt so much more comfortable, happy to be the poor girl myself again, the one without the store-bought dresses and expensive toys. I didn't know why it made me feel so good.

—*Joanna Katherine Wiebe*

CHAPTER FOUR

Tell a Story—Better Still, Tell Many Stories

You can choose no better way to write your memoirs than by telling many, many stories. Some exposition, or explaining, will be necessary, but stories delight the hearts of all readers and are the main reason they are willing to plow through pages of factual material. Your reader can relate to stories. Stories explain the truths of life better than many long sermons.

Without knowing it, you tell stories every day. At the dinner table you may start out, "A funny thing happened to me today on the way to the office." And then you reproduce for your family what happened in such a way they laugh, cry, or exclaim with you. Through a story you help another person to move into your world. You give that person a sense of belonging not achieved through exposition or reasoning. Stories are a form of knowing and of passing on knowledge. In earlier times the elders of a tribe or community explained with a story why the bear sleeps all winter and why the snake sheds its skin. Later generations told their children stories of what happened the year of the big snow or the time a prairie fire

swept through the village. And, in the telling, an aware-
ness of life and its hurdles and rewards are conveyed to
the listeners.

What is a story? A story has to do with events in time,
with life in motion. Stories are specific. Something hap-
pens (an action) to someone (character) in place and time
(setting), perhaps illustrating some comment or reaction
to life (theme). The purpose of a story or narrative is
usually to entertain, to inform, or to illustrate a principle
or support an argument. A large portion of the Bible is in
narrative form. Christ told many stories to His disciples
and followers. The Old Testament carries many accounts
of life in motion, and these are the parts we read to
children and enjoy ourselves because they tell us about
God's dealings with ordinary people.

A well-told story has certain characteristics:

1. It must cover a unit of time, a period complete in itself, not just a fragment.

2. It should focus on a meaningful series of events,
held together by some theme, so that when you're
finished your audience doesn't say, "So what?" A story is
not just the telling of a random collection of events, such
as "I went downtown, bought some groceries, had the
car filled with gas, and took a letter to the post office."
This account includes a sequence of connected actions,
and covers a complete unit of time, but is not yet a story.
However, if I were to tell you that before I went
downtown I looked for the family cat but couldn't find it,
and after all my errands had been done and I had parked
the car, the cat crawled out from under the hood, I have
a story because I have added the element of tension. The
episode with the cat explains why I was reciting the
details of the morning's errands: A cat has nine lives; my

story proved it again. A story must have a point.

3. A story or narrative usually has a certain pattern. It has a beginning section or introduction, which gives the setting or the situation. For a short narrative, don't make this part long; but it should give a minimum of information about where the story is taking place, when, and who the main characters will be, and enough of the conflict (tension) to show there is a line of development ahead. It should also create the emotional atmosphere as serious or humorous. But don't let the cat out of the bag (or hood) too soon. Don't begin the cat story with "This morning the cat accompanied me downtown under the hood of the car." With that beginning, you don't have to tell the rest.

The middle part of your story includes the action. This section is usually a series of events in which the tension grows in intensity. You sense the story is heading for a crisis of some kind. It may be only a very mild crisis like a sneeze or a fish that got away, or it may be a big event like the birth of a baby in the cab of a truck, or a tornado.

The ending of your story is not just the end of the action, b . when the action achieves its full meaning, or when all the forces in the narrative have worked themselves out. When you have finished telling your story, quit writing. Don't keep explaining and moralizing. Let your reader draw his or her own conclusions.

The secret of good storytelling is to move as close to the experience as possible. Take the reader by the hand and lead him or her through the happening. Work like a photographer with a zoom lens. Get so close that you can help them experience exactly what it felt like the first time you had the experience. As you write, ask yourself questions related to the senses. What did it look like?

What did I hear at the time? What did I smell, taste, and feel?

Years ago when I was about ten or eleven, I went to a summer resort with my aunt and uncle and sister. In the pool I tried to reach the center island, though I could not swim. As the water got deeper, I lost touch with the bottom. I was certain I was drowning. How did I feel physically? The acrid water cut my nose and throat as I gulped for air. I grasped for something solid, but each time my hands plunged forward to grab the railing, they came back empty. How did I feel inside? I was angry with myself for trying such a foolish stunt. I was frightened. What would my parents say if I drowned? I was humiliated because I had finally met something I could not master, and therefore I refused to holler for help. I was desperate, but didn't know what to do. Yes, I reached the center island and made it back to the side rails. But why didn't I ever tell anyone about the incident? Clearly, my embarrassment was too great, and I hid the incident deep inside me until I could face this childhood failure.

As you write, take time to think about the sounds of home when you were a child. A night, after the family had retired, what did you hear before you too drifted off? In our wooden, two-story dwelling with its small bedrooms, each night I listened for the downstairs clock to chime the quarter hour at least once. At times I felt compelled to stay awake until the hour struck, but I didn't always make it.

Around me, sisters and brother coughed and turned in their beds, coil springs creaking. If the weather was cold, the frost popped the nails in the siding like a machine gun. Sometimes the wind howled around the corners of the house with brutal force. In the distance, a dog howled, and I remembered with a start the ghost stories in which dogs howling meant spirits of the past were stalking the present. I crawled deeper into the comforter, but not so deep I couldn't hear the fire crackling ever so gently in the big pot-bellied heater downstairs. Occasionally a log fell to the grate in ashes, its energy used up. Or a piece of ice was forced to let go its hold of the side of the water tank in the kitchen, and slid to the bottom with a quiet splash.

In the early mornings of summer, when the windows were flung open, next door the neighbor blacksmith prepared his shop for the day's work. Tools clanged against the anvil. An early customer was waiting for him. Across the street a shopkeeper who lived down the street was already stomping to work on the wooden sidewalk. Sometimes he stopped to greet a passerby. Before long, I knew, the Catholic church bell would call its parishioners to early mass. Seven twenty-five. A meadowlark cried jubilantly that daylight had come. An early fly buzzed by the open window. Then I knew, even before I heard her words, Mother would say, *"Kinder, Zeit zum Aufstehen."* And my bare feet would hit the bedroom floor with a thump.

As you write, aim at telling the story, not telling *about* the story. Show rather than tell. Here is an example of telling about an incident that happened long ago. It has since become a standing family joke.

When I was about sixteen I enjoyed playing the piano. One day, my father, who liked to listen to folk songs, invited a neighboring minister to join us for the evening. After we had sung a while, the man kissed me slyly. Dad didn't like it, so he made sure the man got home that night and never came back.

Now here is the same story to show what actually happened that night. Notice it includes a beginning, a middle, and an ending. I have kept the number of characters to a minimum, although the actual event included other characters, to show Dad and the Welshman as the main characters in tension regarding their values.

My Father and the Welshman

My father loved good singing. He was also a man of great generosity. Taken separately, these characteristics were each his great strength. At those times when he exercised them together, they proved to be his great weaknesses.

Some of my best memories as a child are connected with the occasions when we, as a family, indulged in an outing. With the prospect of a fairly long drive before us, perhaps 20 to 40 miles, it was not long before Father's fairly ordinary baritone filled the 1925 McLaughlin-Buick with song. The car was full already—two adults and five children—but Father's singing always made the itchy closeness of my sister Annie's sweater seem less disagreeable and the cramped quarters which included my feet, the picnic hamper, and a jump seat for little Susie, seem less confining. As his voice rang out with "There's a church in the valley by the wildwood," we children chimed in with "Come, come, come to the church in the wildwood," in the chorus.

Father was also a generous man. He enjoyed giving of himself, his time, his money, his earthly possessions. I have known him to accept a string of fish in payment for groceries and then carry them out the back door to the garbage heap because he didn't like cleaning them. And

Mother didn't either! But he had saved the man's pride. Years after I left the community, I returned one day to the streets where I had spent so many of my growing years. I dropped in at the shoemaker shop; the proprietor was a newcomer to the village, but he knew my father. I told him who I was. "That man never had an enemy in his life," he said. I knew Father as the champion of the underdog, the minorities, the poor, the unsuccessful, the unemployed. He believed strongly in hospitality for everyone.

One day he came home from the s ore to tell us he had met the young minister from the neighboring community and had asked him to come over some evening to sing. Father loved to hear good singing. One evening a young, rotund Welshman came to the house to spend the evening singing for Father. Father enjoyed it immensely. He told the Welshman to come back again.

But father had forgotten he had three daughters all in their middle teens. He probably thought of us as young and innocent and the minister as old and beyond the foolishness of doing what comes naturally.

New Year's Eve brought the young man to our home again. He had been visiting parishioners in our community and had clearly toasted the season once too often. My father, a teetotaler who wouldn't even eat fruitcake baked with brandy, was filled with consternation at the situation, but his love for singing won out. Our staid old parlor rollicked to such tunes as "Wait Till the Cows Come Home, Maggie," and "When It's Springtime in the Rockies." I played the piano and the Welshman sang.

All went well until our guest sang, "Drink to me only with thine eyes," with such deep emotion in his voice that Dad got fidgety. This was something else he had not reckoned with. His plans for his daughters did not include country ministers of another denomination. His enjoyment of the singing grew noticeably less as the evening drew on and the young minister's enthusiasm for me increased. He helped me find the page numbers. He bent over me ever so gently when the book would not stay in place, and held it there with one hand. The other hand lay gently on my shoulder. When he sang, "K-k-k-katy, beautiful Katy," he sneaked in a kiss on my cheek. Dad looked very worried.

This golden-voiced tenor marched through song after song in the *Old Favorites Songbook*. It was late, at least ten o'clock, when he finally gave in and decided it was time to drive home. We children trooped upstairs to bed. From our window facing the street, we listened as he tried to start his old car. The starter whined and whinnied, but the engine would not turn over. The weather was bitterly cold, about 20 degrees below zero.

"He can't get his car started," shouted little Susie to Mother and Father from the top of the stairs. "He's coming back to the house." Our singer knocked at the door, sheepish, apologetic. He couldn't get the car started. The battery had either gone dead or else the gas line was frozen. Could he stay for the night?

Father was nonplussed. I never knew what he thought at that moment, but I could imagine. If our friend spent the night he would probably also spend New Year's Day with us. The hour was late. Father was sleepy, and this young man was on his hands through his own doing. Yet he had never turned anyone out of his home before. Mother stood behind him listening to the conversation, not saying a word. We watched from the stairs.

My father is no mechanic, but he put on his sheepskin-lined mackinaw and offered to help the Welshman get his car started, so he could go home to the comfort of his own bed.

Many minutes later, Father came in elated. The car had started. The singer would make it home that night. But that ended the parlor singing nights in our home.

In writing these stories, give people names. In this story I have called our guest "the Welshman." In some instances you may not wish to identify them all by their right names, but it is easier for your reader to keep track of your characters if they have names instead of reference such as "this certain woman," "my teacher," "the boy next door," and so forth. Give your parents, grandparents, aunts, and uncles names also. Too many nameless aunts running through a story are hard to keep separated. Not everyone who will read your memoirs will be well acquainted with all your relatives. You may use relational terms to speak of family members, but make sure the reader knows whom you are referring to. It used to be customary for husband and wife to call each other "Mama" and "Papa" or forms of these words in the presence of or for the sake of the children. These then sometimes became their names for one another in private also. In a story about your life, your reader may become confused if you refer to a spouse as Mama or Papa and to your actual parents with the same terms. For the sake of clarity, you may have to give up one set of such terms and use given names or terms like Grandma Wiebe and Grandma Funk.

What kinds of stories should you write about? Write about critical incidents with strong emotional overtones, such as deaths, births, illnesses, happy times and crises in home and community life, migration and work experiences. But don't omit the little stories about your first encounter with a stray dog or why you never learned to ride a bicycle.

Write a series of stories related to childhood, adolescence, and young adulthood. Childhood is usually a series of high and low events, of embarrassments and victories, and of times of being either a hero or a fool. Can you recall what happened the first time you went fishing, your first date, your first day at work, your first track meet, your first train ride, your first attempt at milking a cow?

Write stories about times you had fun as a family and times you children were sick together. Tell about the time your mother, firmly convinced sick people should fast, sent you to bed without supper but with an onion poultice on your chest for your cough, and you got so hungry you ate the poultice. Tell stories about courting and marrying and having families. Who were your heroes and role models? Who were the villains in the community whom you were admonished to avoid? Tell stories of how these people influenced your life.

It helps to write the story down the first time as fast as you can without worrying about the final effect. As you go over it a second time, add more details. Describe what was happening more fully. Was your teacher ugly and stout, or slim and beautiful? What color was her hair? When you describe the classroom, don't forget the map case on the wall, the smell of the blackboards and the white chalk buried in shavings, the feeling of emptiness in the pit of your stomach before the noon bell rang, the color of the girls' hair ribbons and the clumsiness of the boys' boots, the fun you had playing street hockey with a piece of frozen horse dung each day after school.

Add details which show your feelings of fear, pleasure, and pain as you write about childhood summers in church camp, on the farm, or in town, wondering what to do. Recall again that wonderful feeling of nakedness when you rolled down your long lisle or woolen stockings for the first time, into brown doughnuts around your ankles, and let the spring breeze caress your white legs.

Don't forget that all-consuming passionate first love of adolescence and your pounding heart as you waited impatiently by the gate after supper for that certain someone to whistle "Mexicali Rose" and hoped that, later, the evening would include a first kiss and another smell of his brand of shaving lotion. As you write, answer the question you think may be in the mind of the reader. What questions do you have after reading this story of a boy's encounter with his father:

Cutting Humiliation

Most adolescents react resentfully to depersonalization. I was no exception when my father wanted to set in my mind the older generation's tradition of a conventional, conformed hair length. I felt strongly that I was old enough to decide this matter for myself. As a typical parent, my father was deeply hurt that his one and only son was rejecting even one value with which he had brought me up. He obviously sensed a need to defend his words just as I refused to back down from my convictions that my hair was my property to do with as I liked. Words did not satisfy our tempers, and soon our lack of communication exploded in a hand-to-hand struggle, and I found myself sitting in a chair in the kitchen with a cloth around my neck. Cluster by cluster, my hair fell among my tears. I was infuriated! The whole younger generation had lost a major battle against tyranny. Humiliation was descending upon my shoulders like boulders. I felt depersonalized, for my own opinion has been spat upon.

What difference do you think it made to this young man to have written about his experience? Or to me that I told you about my near-drowning as a child?

Here are some ideas to get you thinking about stories you have to tell:

1. What was one way your family had fun together? Do you remember any one occasion more clearly than the others because of something that happened?

2. Who is one person you admired as a child or young person and why?

3. How did you celebrate your birthdays? Were you ever the birthday child?

4. How did courting take place? What were your feelings about what was happening to older brothers and sisters when someone came calling?

5. When visitors came to your home, what were some of the things which took place? Who visited your home often? What did you eat that was different? What were your feelings when you had company?

6. Did you ever feel lonely or set aside at home? at school? at church? How did this happen?

7. What were some of the activities which were taboo in your home and community? Can you think of any particular incident in regard to some of these questionable activities? Did you ever take part in them?

8. What kinds of work did you have to do as a young person at home? Did you enjoy this work?

9. How did you and your brothers and sisters get along? What made life hard or easy living with them?

10. What kinds of pranks did you play on each other?

11. Describe a skill you tried to learn as a youngster. What happened? Were you proud of yourself? How did other members of the family react?

12. Describe a place you connect with your childhood, such as playhouse, pasture, barn, empty lot. What events took place there? Who was with you? How did you feel about that place as a child? How do you feel about it now?

Here are some comments I made on some narratives written by a group of students over sixty writing about their past. The comments may give you some help in shaping your memoirs.

—Can you share a little more about the agony and bitterness of that early school experience? Why didn't the other children accept you? Was it because you couldn't speak English? How did the other boys mistreat your brother? Was it with words or physically? Why was he picked out for mistreatment? You make the reader curious when you do not give some of this information.

—Move more slowly through your story. Stop to let the reader know who the people are, where the story is taking place, and so forth. In other words, stop to tell the story. How old were you when the incident happened? Where did it take place in relationship to what you were writing about previously? Was it on a farm? In town?

—You may want to say something more about what the school looked like, about fun at lunchtimes, what you brought along to eat, games you played at recess, Christmas programs and other kinds of programs, what kinds of clothes you wore to school, what chores you had to do at home, how much homework you had to do and where you did it.

—How can you write about a childhood religious experience so your grandchildren will read it and know what was taking place in your mind? Write your experience so that it is uniquely yours, and no one else could write his or her name above it. This will mean avoiding religious clichés and adult terminology ("the Holy Spirit brought me under conviction"). These are all terms you learned later on. What kinds of feelings and thoughts did you have as a child as you considered what you should do with Christ?

—Early Christmas experiences are always good to write about because they reveal many rich and fulfilling experiences. You have a good outline here. Now add more detail. For example, when did this happen? Where? Why were you poor? Because of the depression or other events? Can you explain a little more about your grandparents' house? What were your feelings as you entered it for Christmas dinner? Did you walk there or ride? I could go on with these questions, but this may be enough to show you how you can make a piece of writing longer and fuller so that it conveys more of what happened then.

Here is a longer narrative which I could have condensed into a few pages or lengthened almost to book-length, because each aspect of the story opens up the door to all kinds of other experiences which formed the warp and woof of our life in that immigrant community of Blaine Lake:

Guests, Banya, and Bedbugs

Guests in our home were fairly common. Mother and Dad believed in hospitality like a farmer believes in rain. Both tend toward good results, usually. Many times my parents entertained strangers who were angels unawares, but when the visitors brought with them other guests which multiplied rapidly when they crawled out of the woodwork, the whole matter took on a different aspect.

Our house was small: we four sisters slept in one small room with sloping ceilings and walls, all calcimined a delicate, feminine pink. The room contained two white iron bedsteads with coil springs. They creaked when we moved despite earnest efforts to stop their creaking. We learned to sleep quietly or incur the wrath of other members of the family. A small dresser with a mottled mirror, shared by all four of us and with a drawer for each one, a table with some wooden chairs, and some braided rugs completed the furniture.

My brother luxuriated in a room to himself, the walls of which were painted a strong masculine blue. My parents in the third small bedroom shared it in winter with an indoor chemical toilet, because the chimney for venting it, unfortunately, was located in their room.

The small central hallway ended in a closet for the clothing of all seven members. Each person had only one extra set of clothing usually, so the closet was never very full. A small linen closet occupied a corner in the girls' room. A stovepipe, gilded with aluminum paint, marched straight up from the downstairs heater through a small opening in the hallway. An open register in the open area in our bedroom to circulate the air completed the heating arrangements. We children found the latter extremely convenient for silent listening to adult conversations carried on past our bedtime in the living room below. We knew the best stories were always told after our bedtime and dealt with more interesting matters than new shoes for Jakie or the neighbor's hollyhocks.

Mother enjoyed company. She thrived on cooking and baking even though the extra guests meant much added work. Planning a meal for company was always a major decision and a full-scale cooking operation. Later, she always remembered exactly what she had served when the occasion was mentioned: "When Abe Friesens came, I served my pork roast with potatoes and gravy. . . ." This was followed by some comment on how the meal had turned out. Usually it had turned out well. The compliments on her cooking were many over the years.

Each batch of guests meant considerable readjustment in sleeping arrangements for us children, for we had no guest room. The brown leatherette couch downstairs opened into a bed for two people. If more had come, in summer we children were sent to the playhouse behind the garage or were laid on a comforter on the floor to look for sleeping comfort. The hard wooden floor made it hard to find sleep or comfort.

Guests came in three categories: relatives and friends; church workers; and strangers of Mennonite origin, although not necessarily of that inner persuasion. To have experienced life on the steppes of the Ukraine was sufficient to qualify for guest privileges. Some barely made it. Dad had to pass the livery barn each evening on the way home from the store where he worked. If he saw a family, particularly with women and small children, planning to bed down in the barn for the night, they ended up at our place, Mennonite or non-Mennonite. They were human beings in need of a bed. Dad often paid the livery stable fee for the travelers' horses as well. "They had no money," was his excuse, and the horses had to be liveried. That he had little money either didn't count.

In summer, some visitors came with only a small suitcase; in winter, others arrived with sheepskins and horse blankets in the early darkness of the long winter night in northern Saskatchewan. These they draped onto the living room linoleum to stay warm for the next day's journey. Some nights the house was so full of human and animal smells and all kinds of sounds, I could almost feel the population explosion.

But guests could be further categorized. One kind came only for a meal or two, usually Sunday dinner and *Faspa*—a light afternoon lunch at which one partook heavily of many cups of coffee, *Zwieback* (a two-decker roll), and endless cookies and pieces of cake and much conversation. Adults were always served first while the children played outside. Often, as I waited on the table when I grew older, I watched with consternation as the cake plate was emptied and refilled and emptied again, and I realized that once again I would not taste Mother's chocolate layer cake with date filling and thick, fluffy chocolate frosting unless I hid a piece under a bowl in the kitchen cabinet. I still recall the heartbreak when I saw a guest take the last piece of chocolate pie—and he had already had one—knowing some of the children outside wouldn't even find out there had been a pie. (I should perhaps explain that visitors had a strange way of multiplying unexpectedly, and a hostess, although she tried to prepare adequately, was never sure of the final head count.)

The second kind of guests came for a meal and a *Banya* (sauna bath). These guests made certain they arrived on Saturdays when the bath was fired up. Our *Banya* squatted comfortably on the corner of our yard, and for a time played an important part in our lives. It cannot be given full tribute in a few short paragraphs, but needs at least a brief explanation to complete the story of the guests. We children heard the virtues of steam baths extolled long before we owned one. Our parents had used them in Russia for decades.

One summer day some men dragged a small, elderly building onto the far edge of the yard with horses and a skid. Next, a carpenter arrived and rearranged the insides of this building into three small rooms. The anteroom served as a dressing room and contained the opening for the oven, the wood supply, a bench, and coat hooks. A small inner room contained the stone-covered barrel-heater and tiered benches where the actual sweating and scrubbing was done. Another room was there because the dimensions of the original building were a little on the large side. It became just a room.

We children never fully appreciated the exotic and erotic characteristics of our *Banya*. I can remember Mother's wry smile when couples returned from its three rooms after a rather lengthy stay, but I assumed they bathed like we did—by turns. I did glean from the discussion among the adults that a session in it cleansed the inner being as it opened the pores of the skin and released the grime from the outer layers of the body. Dad believed in steam baths almost as much as he believed in God. When one finished the steam bath ritual of sweating and washing, one should be able to burst forth into the brisk outer air shouting "Hallelujah" as if one's sins had been newly forgiven.

When we girls bathed, we went through the motions somewhat perfunctorily, sitting on one of the three benches with our little basin of water for the prescribed ten or fifteen minutes for a short or long sweat. My sister Annie insisted horses sweated, men perspired, and women glowed; but I found I could sweat without embarrassment in the *Banya* when Annie or Frieda poured water on the stones to create a new head of steam. After a few minutes on the lowest bench, we moved to a higher level as we became acclimatized to the heat. Then we quickly washed and dried our sweaty little bodies, jerked back into our clothes, and dived into the freer air outside, glad when it was summer and groaning in winter when the frigid air hit us. The urge to close the pores quickly, which obsessed some of the adults, didn't concern us.

A thin plank sidewalk made a direct beeline for the back alley, from the kitchen door of the house. At the garden, it angeled sharply to the left to the neighbor's fence, following it around until it reached first the *Banya* and then the outhouse—another one of our outbuildings worthy of much more than a few paragraphs. It served both family and guests adequately, especially in summer.

The outhouse had many uses besides the one for which it was built, including reverie, reading, and retreat from doing dishes or similar disagreeable chores. The call of nature always came conveniently, and who could deny the matter was pressing? Each week the multi-colored privy (odds and ends of paints were used to protect it from the elements during depression times) was scrubbed, and for half a morning the door of Funks' outhouse hung open to allow it to dry, and thereby showing the passing world its rack of reading material. Mother kept it well supplied with religious literature and other informational material essential to the development of growing children, especially anything concerning the birds and the bees. She knew our insatiable appetite for reading and what we'd do if we found ourselves regularly confined to a small space and confronted with her selection of reading. This material was changed periodically. Only strangers to the family were bewildered when we nonchalantly said at suppertime, "I read in the toilet this morning that. . . ."

Beneath the reading shelf was the supply of orange and apple wrappers if the season was right, newspaper squares if it wasn't, and the mail-order catalog with its slick full-color pages for extreme situations when no one was in calling distance to bring more and better paper.

In broad daylight we skipped and jumped our way along the narrow boardwalk to the back. Life was sunlight and new tender carrots to munch as we fulfilled our mission. We pulled the carrots from the garden as we sauntered past. The first person out in the morning picked the ripe raspberries from the branches hanging over our yard from the neighbor's patch. On the return trip to the kitchen we were supposed to bring back an armful of wood.

In the darkness of night we felt each step carefully, berating the sister who had forgotten to put the flashlight back into its accustomed place in the kitchen cabinet. At all times of the day, if we had played too long and too hard, and the call of nature was obeyed too late, the trip to the back was a gymnastic feat of both daring and courage. It was personal disaster to fail. As we staggered back, we clutched our clothing frantically, discarding coats and belts without regard to where they landed, in a panic to make it to the two-holer in time. These items were retrieved on the return journey. Guests made the same pilgrimage, but more sedately.

To the meal and steam bath guests I must add the bed guests. These included friends and relatives, preachers, evangelists, vacation Bible school workers, and sometimes complete strangers. They might come for a day to a week.

Preachers came in many varieties, each one adding to our treasury of memories. I remember well an elderly minister who identified himself to us children as "*der Mann mit dem geflückten Bauch*" (the man with the patched belly). I often wonder if, when he took off his clothes at night, his abdomen displayed a vulcanized patch the way the inner tubes of the car did after Dad had fixed them. The man explained to us that he had had stomach surgery and needed a special diet. Mother conscientiously cooked special meals for him all week. On Sunday our guest with the patched bodyworks went to the Russian Baptist church in the country and enjoyed with the others a carry-in dinner not equaled by modern church potluck meals. What loaded down the table, he sampled. That night he was ill. "What did you eat?" queried Mother. "Head cheese," he replied. Dad rushed to find the doctor to save the preacher from a premature demise. The next day he sat outside in the sun, his shirt open to allow the sun to warm his innards. I didn't see him, but he embarrassed my sister no end, for sunbathing was as yet not in her thinking as part of the activity of elderly gentlemen.

The strangers in our home included those of the casual Mennonite category who came from up north. They had found the long isolation unbearable and were making their annual trek across the frozen river to the Mennonite settlements on the other side. The two-day journey by horse and sleigh was broken at Blaine Lake. Winter weather in Saskatchewan can be cruel to animals and people, yet the drivers trotted the horses into town, breath steaming, heavy fur frosted, and bells jingling. The animals were bedded down in the livery barn, and the tiny cutters and cabooses—pouring forth smoke from their tiny heaters—clustered around the barn like chickens around a mother hen, but all pointing their tongues in the same direction. Some of the owners of these tiny closed-in sleighs spent the night at our place. Each of us children carries a few memories of guests of this category we enjoyed and those we could do without. Annie remembers one woman who did her a good deed. She was learning to knit for a school project. The visitor, having nothing to do that evening, finished Annie's knitting project before she went to bed. The next morning my sister could take the completed project to school way ahead of schedule.

This pattern of hospitality continued unabated for several years. Then suddenly it changed. After a series of overnight guests who had brought loads of their own bedding into the house, we girls came down mornings with large, itchy, red welts on our bodies. Mother was horrified. She didn't want to say the horrible word of what our condition was out loud. She thought "that" had been left far behind in Russia. We were instructed to tell no one of the terrible things that had come to pass at the poor, but respectable, Funk household. Bedding was boiled and washed. Mattresses were painstakingly searched, sprinkled with a special insecticide, and the bedrooms thoroughly cleaned and recalcimined. But not every crack yielded up its residents. Some had come to stay. So the bedbugs lived on, and we girls continued to itch and squirm.

That summer that part of the house was locked tightly and all window and door cracks sealed with strips of newspaper. The oldest mattresses were taken to the village dump and burned. For a week we children slept in the playhouse and Mother and Dad slept in the lean-to kitchen while the fumes of burning sulphur cleansed the house of all inhabitants. That ended one problem successfully.

But Mother was concerned about the bedbugs returning. One evening Dad came home in the late afternoon as we children arrived home from school. An older couple with a grandchild was passing through town. Could they spend the night with us? Mother agreed. She prepared supper for them as usual, but only many years later did I find out what really happened that night.

"Where will you put them to sleep?" Dad had asked. She'd find a place for them, she said. Mother made up Dad's and her bed (now on the dining room couch) for the guests to use. That night she slept with one of us girls in our bedroom and my youngest sister slept on the floor. She told Dad he would have to sleep with my young brother Jakie for the night. This arrangement was a brand-new one, but Dad didn't complain. He understood her concern about bringing unknown guests upstairs and reintroducing the bedbugs.

After everyone had settled down, Mother said she could hear Dad muttering to himself in the tiny bedroom across the hall about the stench caused by Jakie's woolen socks and moccasins, stiff with perspiration, waiting to be put on again the next day. They rested calmly beneath the bed, close to Dad's nose. In winter, because we had to melt snow and ice for water for all purposes, we bathed only once a week and changed socks not much oftener.

Dad often claimed he didn't perspire. My brother, however, could not make the same claim. We all knew differently each night when he removed his socks. Dad covered the offending items with his clothes. No use. He moved them farther under the bed. The acrid odor of several days' perspiration hung heavy in the small room. Sleep was impossible. Finally, he opened the window and flung the socks and moccasins far out into the snow. Then he slept.

Mother chuckles when she tells the story, and Dad grins and looks sheepish. The next winter the flow of guests dried up. Possibly Dad didn't want another encounter with my brother's socks. The reason may also have been that cars began to replace horse-drawn vehicles, making it possible for the long journey across the river to be made in one day.

CHAPTER FIVE

Fill Your Memoirs with People

Bran muffins are definitely more interesting with raisins in them. Writing which includes mention of people is also more inviting. Rudolph Flesch in *The Art of Readable Writing* has worked out a system for measuring human interest in writing by counting the words which name people, their relationships, and pronouns referring to them in successive samples of 100 words. The larger the number of personal words, the higher the human-interest factor of the piece of writing.

People not only add interest, but are also an important link to the past. The history of a nation is in large part the story of those individuals who had a part in shaping that story. The account of your life is likewise a portrayal of how your life touched the lives of others and how you were influenced by them. Someone has said we are an omnibus in which our forefathers ride. That omnibus should also include seats for friends, teachers, pastors, and casual acquaintances. You can't talk about school experiences without naming those who sat on the same schoolbench with you. You can't tell how you decided to become a teacher or what teaching was like without introducing the persons who influenced you to become a teacher.

When the periodical *People,* published by *Time,* appeared, the editors said it was all about "winners, losers, lovers, dreamers, and other human beings . . . caught in the act of being themselves." They said they had gotten their idea from the Bible, a book also about winners, losers, lovers, dreamers, and other human—very human—beings. They were probably thinking of persons like Jacob, Joseph, Solomon, Rachel, Miriam, Peter, and John. Can you imagine the Bible without any people in it, no stories—only sermons, prayers, and explanations of ideas? Hardly.

Travelogs become more interesting and valuable when they include encounters with persons the traveler has met. Similarly, your memoirs become more interesting and worthwhile if they include stories of people you encountered along the way, sometimes only for a few minutes, sometimes over a period of many years. But do not pick out only important persons such as teachers, church and civic leaders. One of Helen Keller's biographies brought out only the large number of celebrities in her life—kings, queens, statesmen, officials—even though she had many friends from all walks of life and had helped many handicapped people. One critic of the book said, "This was not a true biography. This book does not quote a single one of the blind, deaf, crippled, poverty-stricken, aged, lonely, to whom Helen Keller was more important than successful people." So your story will not be true if you pick out only the time you shook hands with the President or rode in the same plane with Billy Graham or Frank Sinatra. Make mention of the little people you met along the way—schoolmates, children, relatives, fellow workers, as well as the occasional enemy. Anyone you had fun with, cried with, admired, or who moved your life along even the tiniest distance should be included.

In your writing include not just what you remember about people, but the way you remember them and the way they affected you. I remember that one of our neighbors was an alcoholic; his wife was a tired old woman. Nearly every Saturday evening he staggered home from the local poolroom and tavern. Sometimes he didn't make it all the way and flopped into the ditch beside the slatted sidewalk. His wife would come out scolding and crying, then set out to find her nearly grown-up sons to help her carry their father home to sleep it off. Often she trudged slowly across the street to tell my mother about her husband and to reach for sympathy. I remember the feeling of curiosity which overcame me, as we children gawked at the little old man lying limp in the gutter. But a kind of sadness was an even stronger emotion. If this was the result of drinking, I didn't want it.

Here are two ways to help you bring people into your memoirs. First, try to remember a moment when some strong feeling, perhaps of anger, resentment, love, thankfulness, enabled you to see an adult clearly. Relive the event in your mind, then capture on paper the circumstances of the incident you recall.

Second, write a case history of the person. Answer these questions about the individual if you are planning on a fairly lengthy sketch:

1. Name, date of birth, place of birth (if you know them).

2. Where did this person grow up? In what kind of surroundings?

3. Who were the other members of the family?

4. Do you know something about the person's schooling or occupation?

5. What kind of clothes did he or she wear? What were some outstanding mannerisms and speech patterns?

6. How did he or she relate to other persons? To you?

7. Describe your character physically with full details.

8. Describe some of the person's mental traits, likes, hates, aims in life, attitudes, and moods.

9. Did he or she have any particular personal problems? Were they overcome?

10. Make a list of all experiences you can recall that involve this person, including the last illness and death. What was it like in your home when this person was ill? Was the person in the hospital or at home? How did the illness and death affect the family? Who told you the person had died? How did you feel then?

Preparing such a case history will help you establish the pattern of a person's choices and behavior—those distincitve peculiarities which set that individual apart from other persons. Was he or she a pillar of the church or the town drunk? The PTA leader or hard-core relief recipient? What kind of person was this individual as you saw him or her? What you saw will likely also say something about yourself, for as you reveal what recurring qualities you noticed in other people, you indicate what you value in life. A person usually sees what one is looking for. If you look for kindness in others, you will find it. If you look for greed, it will match your own.

In writing about other people in your memoirs, you do not have to account for their behavior—the reasons, for example, for irrational or even extravagant or irresponsible behavior of parents, brothers and sisters, and friends. The traumas of life are always with us. You may know why your parents didn't let you stay out later than ten o'clock but not why a teacher had an uncontrollable temper. So explain the first if you can and simply record the second.

As you write, record not only the facts about what happened in your contacts with people, but also the truths behind them. Were your parents the first in the churchyard each Sunday morning though they lived the farthest away? Were they concerned about keeping their own yard tidy? What did their faces look like when you brought home your report card? a torn dress or pants? a bouquet of flowers? What do your answers tell about their character?

One way of handling this material is to state clearly what influence someone had on you, and then follow it with a series of specific incidents which account for that influence. This is the traditional topic sentence/example type of writing you learned in grade school. Don't explain too much. Once again, show rather than tell. It is better to guide the reader to what you want him or her to think about the person, and let the material speak for itself. Here are two short paragraphs to give you some idea of what I mean:

> Though money was always in short supply in our home and, as a family, we had our share of quarrels and laughs, I grew up feeling secure about my parents. When I really needed them, I could count on their being around—Mother at home and Father outside the home. One Christmas we children all caught the red measles. The short, stubby doctor came, looked us over, took our temperatures, and left

again. Before he departed, he nailed a hateful isolation sign on the front door. No visitors or visiting for as long as one of us was sick. One by one, we all came down with the measles. Mother patiently nursed each child through to health. One evening I felt too sick to live. Red itchy skin, fever, runny nose, hacking cough, and boredom in that stuffy bedroom had taken their toll. My sister was nearly delirious with fever. That night Mother crawled into bed between her two unhappy, wheezing, sneezing daughters and loved us back to sound health.

Other occasions when I particularly felt this sense of protection and concern occurred when we drove home late at night through the dark. The roads were always rough and rutty. But we were going home. Dad was driving, and Mother sat next to him, usually with one child on her lap and the other arm holding the back door handle on Dad's side so no one would fall out. One by one we four children jammed into the back seat would fall asleep, borrowing a head or shoulder to use as a pillow. We belonged together, to one another. We could sleep, for Father was driving and Mother was watching.

Here is the beginning of a longer sketch about my mother. Each trait mentioned here could be expanded with many additional stories to give it more validity.

My Immigrant Mother

Each morning my father was the one who went out into the world—though the world in Blaine Lake was fairly small. Dad's world included the store, the street, the municipal office, the bank, the post office, some other businesses, and some individuals involved with church and community affairs. Mother stayed at home, and for many years was probably invisible to most of the local inhabitants.

But we children knew she was there. I see her as the core of our home around which everything else revolved. When emotions got tangled (hers included) and tempers flared, she brought matters back to an even keel. She went back into the kitchen and cooked a good meal. We sat down together around the small kitchen table and forgot what had sparked the flareup.

Mother had come from an extremely hard life in Russia, working away from home since preadolescence, first as a *Kindermädchen* (babysitter), then as a hired girl, and later as a cook. She had left behind in Russia much poverty, illness, unsettled living conditions, and most of her relatives, including her parents. The new land would provide better for her family—she was sure of that. She came to North America with a positive attitude. Hard work, thrift, mutual support, and trust in God would make this new life a better one.

She tells me the first winters in Saskatchewan were lived in almost primitive conditions. When their first tiny two-room house in Laird (where I was born) was enlarged to three, "We felt like a king and queen, we were so happy." Other immigrants in the village were still living in chicken coops and saw the Funk home as a mansion. Each Sunday, all winter, they gathered there for food and fellowship. "We needed each other," says Mother.

But like all immigrants, she spoke no English, and so in Blaine Lake she enjoyed little social life with other women, for very few spoke German. "I was very lonely during the first years in Blaine Lake with no one to talk to but Dad," she says.

When we children started school, she read through each primer with us, one by one—not to help us, but to

teach herself to read. She succeeded. By the time I left
high school she could read difficult novels like *Doctor
Zhivago* and enjoy them. Her formal education in Russia
had stopped after three years. Now reading became her
great enjoyment, and she encouraged each of us children
to read good books, and saw to it that we borrowed them
from libraries.

As a family we spoke only Low German until my older
sisters started school in the early thirties. One year
another family (Dad's cousin) arrived from the Old
Country and spent several weeks with us before they
located permanently across the river. That summer vacation my two older sisters lived with this family and attended German school, which Dad's cousin taught. The
family spoke only High German—no English or Low
German. When my sisters returned home, they had a fair
mastery of High German. Mother promised us each a
purse if we would discontinue speaking Low German at
home. We agreed. She knew that the Platt Deutsch, only
an oral dialect, was inadequate for the life ahead. We
would need more than one language. From then on, we
mixed languages in our home like salad ingredients.
Eventually the language situation settled into layers: we
spoke English to our parents; they replied in High
German or English. When they were alone, they
conversed in Low German. And if the subject matter was
highly secret and we might overhear, they switched to
Russian.

In Russia Mother had made her living as a cook and
brought with her to Canada a reputation as an excellent
one. I can recall my brother Jakie standing on top of our
large woodpile after a meal he had particularly enjoyed,
shouting, "My mother is a royal cook, my mother is a

royal cook." And she was. Rolls, cakes, pies, cookies, *Platz*, and other Mennonite delicacies issued from her oven regularly. Through cooking she expressed her creativity. She never merely cooked a meal: she created and gave of herself to others in her cooking and baking. When the local church women's groups held sales, her buns and cakes were in high demand, and sometimes spoken for long before we children carefully carried them to the site of the sale.

Closely aligned to her cooking was her gift of hospitality. A guest must always be offered something—at least a cup of tea and a cookie. Mother may have said "cookie" to express her views, but in actuality, she meant a bountiful plate of cinnamon rolls, crumbcake, or five or six kinds of cookies produced from her storehouse of baked goodies. Throughout the years, when we children came home with spouses and children, we knew we would always receive a royal welcome and lots of royal food, but we didn't shout it from the woodpile like my fat little brother used to. We simply ate and enjoyed it. Mother and food were a twosome no one forgot easily.

She gave away recipes gladly, but the difficulty was to know how to interpret them. She knew by intuition how much of each ingredient to use, especially for those recipes she filed in her head. "Add a good cup of lard," she'd say, for a recipe for *Perishkee*. "What's a good cup of lard?" I'd ask. "Well, good—*good*." She emphasized the word. That emphasis should indicate to me how much. If one had to ask the question, one should not bother making *Perishkee*.

The hard years in Russia, living without many material possessions, kept her detached from her possessions in Canada. Like Dad, she believed in giving to others what she did not need. Even today, my suitcase always travels back with me fuller than when I came. Our gifts to her are frequently returned as an expression of her love after a year or two in her home. Her closets were never cluttered with clothing not being worn. These were immediately carried to the closest poor family. Because my sister and I were much the same size, Mother often made us dresses of the same material and pattern, so that people mistook us for twins. One day I came to school wearing a favorite flowered-print dress. Into the classroom walked the daughter of one of the poorest families in town in a similar dress. She was wearing Annie's outgrown dress, one I'd never wear because I already owned a duplicate. I was twins again—but I didn't enjoy this version.

Perhaps Mother was too protective of us children, particularly in situations which might have taught us to adjust to life's shortcomings. Yet as I think back to some such events, I realize she was always also protecting someone else. One Sunday we motored north to see some friends. North meant venturing into homestead territory where people still lived in dismal poverty without many conveniences and often without enough food or adequate water supply.

While Mother and Dad visited inside, we children stayed in the car. As the woman of the house prepared the evening meal, Mother noticed she was setting out some gooseberry mousse, cooked with milk, and with great lumps of cottage cheese floating in it. Surely this was a cooking disaster! She knew we children would never eat it, but she didn't want us to embarrass her hostess (or herself!). Mother came out to the car to tell us to eat the leftover sandwiches from the breakfast we had brought along, and then she explained to her hostess not to bother setting out food for us children. We had enough to eat in the car. Later she admitted she had found it hard to swallow the meal herself in the sour-smelling, dusty, fly-specked kitchen. If we children had eaten there, it would probably have been from the un-washed plates of the adults, a custom brought along by some people from Russia. However, years later Mother discovered to her chagrin that the dish with the curds the woman had served was supposed to be that way.

We children laugh now at her idiosyncrasies—such as her attitude toward dishwashing and housecleaning:

Maxim No. 1: In her home Mother always washes dishes. When she visits us, she also washes the dishes. This is her job. No amount of talking, arguing, or rea-soning can change her mind about dishes. No woman will ever face Saint Peter and say she had to wash dishes in Anna Funk's kitchen, nor will any woman ever accuse her at the judgment throne of not having been willing to do her share of dishes after she had eaten elsewhere.

Maxim No. 2: Cleanliness is next to godliness. Each spring and fall the house endured a vigorous housecleaning. Each piece of furniture, each curtain, all mattresses and bedding were moved, aired, and cleaned. Walls were washed and chimneys taken down and de-sooted. In ad-dition, every week the house was given a thorough clean-ing from top to bottom, including the playhouse, bath-house, and verandah. Each girl had her responsibilities. My job was to dust furniture, ledges (high and low), and the staircase. I knew every crack, ridge, and hole in all of these items. At times I attempted reading a book in one hand and dusting with the other in unison.

Every Saturday night the family bathed in whatever

amount of water was available. This was, of course, before we acquired the bathhouse. In early years the rites of bathing were conducted in a small round washtub in the center of the kitchen and supervised by Mother. This room was declared off limits for several hours to all but the one bathing. In later years an oblong tub replaced the washtub, and, still later, the tub became a permanent fixture in the partitioned-off bathroom. We carried water to it from the kitchen stove reservoir. It ran out on its own power. Progress.

We always bathed from youngest to oldest, or more bluntly, from cleanest to dirtiest. Each newcomer to the tub could add a half pail of hot water before he or she plumbed the depths of the murky, soap-curdsy mixture. My oldest sister says that to this day she never washes her face in the tub. The conditioning was too strong.

Mother believed in sponge baths for herself. In the afternoon, after the dishes were done, she washed herself, put on a clean dress and apron, and for a short time read her Bible, prayed, read the mail and glanced over the papers. She always sat down to read a letter, for someone had sat down to write it. Letters were important. But she always stood to wash dishes and to cook. To sit at such work revealed laziness.

Mother worked hard to find her identity and place in this strange land with different customs and, at times, difficult adjustments. She struggled to move out of the forced isolation created by language and culture. She attended English church services before she could understand a word. She invited our schoolteachers and wives of local dignitaries—the banker, the doctor, the lawyer—to afternoon teas to show her willingness to become a part of community life. Afternoon tea was a British custom, but she accepted its disciplines gladly.

Years later she joined the local Red Cross, Ladies Aid Society, and similar women's groups and found new opportunities to contribute her work, particularly her skills in cooking and knitting. She never crocheted. She hated to crochet, she said. One day she told me why. When she had been a young woman working on a large estate in Russia, the estate owner's wife had demanded all the hired girls (and there were always many) to put in a full working day—from sunup to sundown. Even if the girls had worked hard physically in the kitchen, in the fields, or in the garden all day, if a few hours of sunlight remained, they were expected to use that time to crochet doilies for the elaborate home.

In the years after Mother learned English, her group of friends grew to include other women besides relatives and German-speaking local residents. She gave encouragement to young married women who were having difficulty with homemaking. She offered moral support to several wives of alcoholics, and gave advice on how to cook and clean to the young wife who could not make ends meet. She prayed for women who faced impossible marital problems. Women came to talk, and though she loved to talk herself, she also listened.

Our home had its share of disturbances. Our parents became discouraged and weary of the struggles of making do, of finding their place in this new land. When Dad was overburdened by business and financial pressures, Mother protected him from us children and our demands. Her loyalty to him was unshakable. At other times, she defended us against his more conservative views and against any and all critics.

Further, she never condemned, blamed, or judged us for

what we had done with our lives and with our spouses and children. Each in-law was a welcome gift.

Within herself she had to find some way, as an immigrant, to adjust to societal changes. She sought to find some balance in this struggle for us children. She allowed Frieda to cut her hair and get a home permanent when the church was still excommunicating women for doing so. She could cite her reasons. She let us wear slacks when Dad couldn't understand our longing to dress like the other girls. When a visiting minister from across the river arrived in town and Dad knew we'd be wearing the offensive garments, he rushed home to tell her to get us girls out of our slacks. She did. She let us wear socks when no one in the Mennonite church wore socks. She persuaded Dad to let us take music lessons and to attend school movies. When Jakie wanted to play pool in the local den of iniquity, because all his friends were congregating there, she let him buy a deck of cards so he could play at home. She often felt the criticism of friends and relatives who were sure her daughters would all marry heathen Englishmen, Doukhobors, or Russians, and depart from the faith. But she believed in prayer, she told them. God would hear her prayers.

Mother had strong opinions on many issues—and told others her views freely—but always out of love for God, the church, or someone near to her. She was staunchly loyal to anyone who had helped her and hers. She was proud to be a Canadian. She spoke of her gratefulness to the Canadian government for allowing Mennonites to enter the country. For decades she faithfully voted for the party which had given permission for their entry into this free land. Yet I recall she also insisted we attend the political rally of the opposition party when the prime minister of Canada visited our community.

She, like Dad, was fiercely independent and found it
hard to ask for help but easy to give it to others. If we
children wanted encouragement, we knew where to go
for it. We knew she and Dad always saw us as winners. In
the last years, she has written few letters, but the knitting
and cooking and cleaning continue. And the concern.

In recent years my brother and sisters have all
celebrated silver wedding anniversaries with gifts and
other festivities. When I visited Mother and Dad one
summer, she pulled out a beautiful cutwork tablecloth
she had purchased. She gave it to me with the words,
"You will probably never celebrate a silver wedding an-
niversary because Walter is gone, but I want you to have
something too." I accepted the gift humbly. As I spread
the table with it, and we as a family gather around it to
eat our meal, I celebrate a mother's love.

CHAPTER SIX

Make It Meaningful

If you were planning to sell your house, how would you describe it? Here are two descriptions of the same house. Which one is more appealing?

For Sale: 3 bdrm., 2 bth., full bmnt., crptd., grge.

For Sale: 3 bedrooms, master with full bath; sunny dining area, wood-burning fireplace in family room; full basement completely finished with large playroom for children; garage has room for workbench; fenced patio; close to schools and stores; large shade trees, circle drive.

If you didn't choose number two, you're probably the kind of person who prefers a tent to a house. The first advertiser used facts only; the second used facts and words with strong positive connotations such as "sunny" and "large" to involve the reader's feelings.

In writing your memoirs, you will want to record facts and dates, but also the way these facts affected you. Involve the reader in the contest of forces which determined your decisions and made you the kind of person you are today. When you add the element of tension, your reader's feelings are caught up in your story sufficiently to say, "Here's a person much like me, who went through the same kinds of experiences of love, hate, fear, hope, joy, sorrow, bitterness, and loneliness, but at different times and under circumstances. But this person survived by the grace of God, and so I can survive also." A reader identifies with meaningful writing. It is hard to identify with cold facts, numbers, and statistics.

How can you bring this element into your writing? If life has had meaning for a person, despite its ambiguities and incongruities, an account of that life will usually have meaning for others also. A true biographer (of one's own life or someone else's) is able to separate the elements in that life that have meaning beyond the many ordinary people who were one's family and friends and beyond the little community in which the person lived, and lay these elements out on the table for all to look at, like a set of photographs. This meaning is usually the essence of that person, what made him or her tick; and when a biographer discovers that quality, he has discovered the person.

If you are the biographer of your own life, when you have discovered what made life meaningful for you, or when you have been able to distill from the myriad experiences of life your value system, you have discovered yourself.

Most people have done a heap of living and collected a heap of goods, such as furniture, house, car, books, dishes, and linens, by the time they have lived out their allotted span of years. Over the same lifetime, the individual also builds up a collection of values, a set of do's and don't's which have helped him or her to make sense out of the world. This collection of values is a person's actual, personal religion, says George F. Simons in *Journal for Life* (Life in Christ). He adds that one's personal religion (or value system) may contain some things inherited and taught by family and church, some things absorbed from the values of society, some things imparted in intimate connections with others, and some things thought and worked out of one's own experiences and reflections.

In sorting out your value system, don't make the mistake of thinking it is necessarily the same as church teachings or even parental teachings. Simons writes that "the experience of religion in individuals and the institutionalization of religion in church teachings, practices of worship and cultural traditions, while often intimately connected, are, in reality, two quite different things." Though you belong to a certain denomination or religion, you actually have your own religion. You and your brothers and sisters may have much in common in your family upbringing and acceptance of a creed, but have different "personal religions." The two are not the same. Though you may both say you believe in the equality of humankind, your actual belief is revealed through your actions and whether you ever mingle with the poor, people of other races, and down-and-outers. You may both openly confess to believing in the creed of your religious group, but your practice with regard to this creed shows what you actually believe. So when you write, you are looking for your personal value system, not the tenets of the faith of your denomination.

In a previous chapter, we spent time thinking about the events of childhood without qualifying what kind of experiences these should be. Writing about what we did when we were young, and where we went, and what happened then is probably the easiest kind of writing. Most of these stories have a great deal of action and, frequently, many characters. But these experiences—the ones which happen so that others can see them—are not the only kind. Many experiences which change our attitudes and values are inner ones. Sometimes you are the only one who knows the joys, hopes, fears, despairs, frustrations, impatience, love, satisfaction, and new courage which moved into your life for a period of time. The event that created this feeling may have been very small—perhaps only a line in a book or poem, a small look of praise from an older friend, a leaf flying in the wind—but its effect on your life was large. How can you bring these inner experiences into the open so that others can understand what you consider some important values in life?

For most people writing meaningfully begins with an impelling urge to systematize their philosophy of life, to unravel the muddle of life, to let others know the felt quality of what life has been.

It continues with a willingness to own the past, regardless of how uncomfortable it may be to return to it, and travel over the same path again, if only in memory. Yet you cannot change the past nor how it influenced you. Sometimes you may be tempted to think of some of the past years as wasted; or even be angry with yourself, with teachers and parents, for what they did or didn't do; or be resentful regarding teachings you accepted from your elders in good faith and which church or society rejects now as no longer valid—for example, a belief that birth control is no longer immoral. Now you see ideas you rejected then because you were taught to reject them, accepted by a society which is changing its values. Yet, as you write, you will soon discover that to accept the past as it was, with all its weaknesses and strengths, is a freeing experience. Once you have owned it as your own, it no longer owns you or controls your feelings. It now belongs to you. You have forgiven as you were forgiven. You can make the past serve you.

So we're back to the question we asked earlier: How can you, a novice writer, make your memoirs meaningful so that people will want to read them? We have mentioned several ways in earlier chapters: tell stories with a point, get as close to the experience as possible (show rather than tell), include people in your writing. Another way is to explain the process by which you arrived at the attitudes you hold toward life. What forces were at work in you throughout the stages of development as you made life choices? Each decision was an expression of a value or attitude. Were these decisions made because of the promptings of jealousy, love, courage, ambition, the desire to be God's person; or were they made because of pressures exerted by public opinion and customs within your community, and by traditions in church, home, and society?

For help in knowing what to write about, answer some of these questions:

What values do you hold regarding school, education, church, money, power, farming, death, other races, camping, sexuality, capital punishment, and so forth?

What did your parents teach you about prayer, salvation, church, spirituality, work, play, wealth, male-female relationships, family, honesty, love, faithfulness?

What was God like as you knew Him? When did you feel

close to Him? When far away? How would you like to know Him? When did you see faith in operation in the lives of other people?

How did you make spiritual decisions? How did you learn about the love of God? About forgiveness? How did you feel about church attendance? About family devotions? Which people in church made you think of kindness?

What were your ways of handling insecurity and complexity? When did you feel safe, cared for, and free from fears of the unknown? When did you feel down, discouraged, desperate, lonely, intimidated, angry, elated, compassionate, liberated?

Why or how did you make some of your choices regarding schooling, vocation, marriage partner, number of children, a place to live, the type of house to live in, automobile, finances?

Did you ever win any awards for special deeds? On the other hand, what are some memories you feel uncomfortable about?

When you have decided on which values you wish to write about, recall specific incidents when you saw this attitude developing. I grew up with a rather uninhibited attitude toward life. Nothing could ever go very wrong for very long. One writer phrases it well for me, "I grew up knowing we were better than no one but infinitely superior to everyone. One succeeded as a matter of course." Only much later in life, because of circumstances, did this free attitude change for a while, but I find loving traces of a strong self-image still with me.

If I planned to write a longer piece about my spiritual pilgrimage, I would first make a list of events which I think have influenced my faith in Jesus as Son of God. This list would include among other details:

Mother reading to us from a German Bible story book each morning and praying with us, thanking God particularly for food, clothing, and shelter. Now as an adult understanding her early experiences, I know why she always mentioned *Kleidung und Obdach* (clothing and shelter).

Going to church in Laird at the Mennonite Brethren Church and also at the United Church, and sometimes at the Russian Baptist. We were ecumenical before we knew it.

Attending street meetings held in Blaine Lake by Salvation Army and other groups.

Attending vacation Bible school during the summer.

Attending revival meetings at the Russian Baptist Church where my sister and I first went forward at an altar call, and the ensuing struggle to fit this into other theological teachings we had encountered.

Memories of Dad's preaching—and also the way he prepared for his ministry.

The church in our home, but of which we children were mostly observers.

The personal dissatisfaction with the way my life was going as a young person, the resulting contact with a group of young Christians, the exposure to literature about the faith-life, and the decision to accept God's truth as truth for me.

With a list like this, I have something to begin with. Next I can add generalizations and anecdotes to fill in and illustrate. The following is an article I wrote about 1965, at the height of the civil rights movement, in which I began as I suggest above—with a list. Then I added details and stories to show the progression in my attitudes toward the blacks. Notice how I use the "Negro" and "colored" terminology which was acceptable at the time. Now, about thirteen years later, I see the article needs another section to bring it up-to-date.

Is the Black Man My Brother?

Someone once told me you can't have convictions on some social issue until you have had personal experience in that area. For instance, you can't really claim an opinion on capital punishment until you have seen a few heads roll, nor can you demand racial tolerance until you have lived with people of other races.

Sometimes I wish my friend's words were true. Then I could get rid of the uneasy feeling that I have the responsibility of coming to some decision in the current race question. I have never seen a man guillotined nor have I had blacks for neighbors. But to say I have no convictions at this time would not be true.

Although I have had very little actual contact with Negroes, I cannot remember at any time in my life when I did not to some extent hold to the opinion that all races were born equal. Although most of my experiences with Negroes have been concentrated within the past few years, my attitudes were molded to a large extent by the attitudes of my father during my childhood.

My father grew up on the steppes of Russia as one of the descendants of the thousands of Mennonite settlers who fled there from Holland and Germany to escape religious persecution. A sturdy, industrious people, many of the Mennonites prospered and became wealthy landowners in their adopted land. They lived aloof in closed Mennonite villages, thereby preserving their own distinct culture quite successfully.

The poor neighboring Russian peasants, not as successful either materially or culturally, became the objects of prejudice on the part of some of the Mennonite settlers. My father's bitter denunciation of this prejudice and his vivid picture of how Russian stable boys were sometimes denied the privilege of even a bed in the attic of the house, but were sent to the hayloft even on cold winter nights, are memories I cannot easily erase.

As the son of a laborer, rather than a landowner, my father sometimes shared the misery of these Russian peasant boys. He learned to love them, but he also formed a basic attitude toward the wealthier or capitalist classes which he carried with him throughout life. He found some things hard to forget. As a young man in his late teens he was forced to attend to complete burial arrangements of four close relatives, among them his own father, during a typhus epidemic which followed a time of famine. Not one of the wealthier people would respond to his plea for help.

I know my father today as one who in his own way has always tried to help those who are being stepped on by others—the poor, the unemployed, delinquents, social outcasts, and similar people. In his seventh decade he added women to this group.

I grew up with stories of the Russian Revolution, not as events which happened in a history book, but the real life experiences of my own parents. As children, we relived the war and the battlefront which moved through the Mennonite colonies, the raids of the Makhnovists, the courage of individuals, and the struggles of all to survive during the famine. It was, therefore, I believe a simple transfer of sympathies from the exploited Russian masses to the discriminated Negroes of the slave era. Mother had read Harriet Beecher Stowe's *Uncle Tom's Cabin* in a German translation. Her account of the slave-girl Eliza's flight over the ice floes with hounds and hunters in full pursuit couldn't be equaled by a "living color" TV production.

And yet I do not think I felt full empathy with the colored people at the time, because in Saskatchewan, Canada, where we lived, we were far removed from the race question as it concerned Negroes. Of course, we did have our Indians, but that was another matter. Indians were simply Indians. They lived on reservations because it was good for them.

Negroes, as we knew them, were but the objects of jest and a source of fun. The only "Negroes" we knew were the jolly minstrels, faces darkened with burnt cork, who gave our recreation-starved community an opportunity to laugh. These were the only "Negroes" we ever knew until one day a strange-looking family moved into the shack at the edge of town: A white man whose youth had long since left him. A white woman, younger than the man, but tired looking and unkempt. And an assortment of children—two white children, two Negro children, black as the night, and one child who was neither black nor white. Their presence in school was both a novelty and a source of embarrassment to us. In early spring when the snow melted and roads opened up, they were gone. I think we were glad.

At about the age of twelve I attended a United Church girls' summer camp. One of the adult leaders was a Negro student from Trinidad. This young woman, who probably knew the meaning of the word "prejudice" more deeply than we young girls grasped at the time, patiently taught us her meaning: *Being down on what you are not up on.* She also taught us her name, syllable by syllable: Wilma Samlallsing. After 25 years lapse of time hers is the only name I remember of more than 100 people I met at that camp.

The experience with the deepest impact on my attitudes to other races, and particularly the Negroes, occurred several years ago when my husband attended graduate school at Syracuse University in Syracuse, New York. I remained in Ontario with our children. Through a friend he found an apartment near the university campus. During the months of his study there he shared this apartment with a Chinese student from Formosa and a young Nigerian, both in America under the sponsorship of the Laubach Literacy Foundation.

Although I met these young men only a few times, my husband shared with me many of the unique experiences of the "little United Nations" housed in that apartment block. We found both of these young men to be intelligent, outstanding individuals. Sometimes it seemed our own American students lacked the caliber of character they displayed on numerous occasions.

Lucky, the Nigerian, more so than Larry, the Formosan, suffered from the blight of racial intolerance. As friends we suffered with him. He related to us how one summer he motored with friends to the West Coast to find summer employment. En route he was denied admittance to some of the restaurants because the proprietors thought he was an American Negro. With the hurt rankling in him, he tested a hunch on the return trip. He traveled the same route and tried to stop at the same restaurants, but there was a difference. This time he was decked out in the outstanding *agbada* of a Nigerian, a long, full-flowing gown of brightly checked cloth, embroidered and closely fitted about the neck. The result: all doors swung open before him.

Together with Lucky we drove through the Negro section of Syracuse. Large, unpainted apartments lay muddled together, with children and adults lolling around on

the rickety outside verandahs. The people looked indifferent and indolent. I couldn't help wondering if the bars
of prejudice which imprisoned them were broken, would
they ever rise to the stature of our friend Lucky?

In recent years, because the race issue is becoming
louder and more insistent. I have tried to look at the
whole matter more rationally, but I realize that books I
have read such as *Black Like Me; Cry, the Beloved
Country; To Kill a Mocking Bird,* are strong opinion
molders.

The church, which has figured very largely in my life,
has not formed as much of my attitude to the race question as it should have, other than to affirm the basic
equality of all persons under God. Perhaps it has spiri-
tualized the matter too much, relating only to the eternal
destiny of Negroes rather than their present needs.

My sister and her family spent about eight years in the
Congo as missionaries. In the recent rebel uprising [early
1960s] they lost all belongings and escaped with only
their lives. My own attitudes were clarified as I read both
church releases and newspaper accounts of the events.
The releases usually emphasized one thing: whether
white people were still safe. The thousands of Congolese
who died in the struggle didn't seem to matter. Whites
were still on top of the heap in matters of life and death,
and the colored races at the bottom.

The full seriousness of the race issue in the United
States almost stunned me when we moved to Kansas
about two years ago. [1962]. In Canada we heard only
the faint rumblings of Negro unrest and discontent, but
now it was a real thing of riots, marches, bombings, and
killings.

Every time I saw a Negro on the streets of Wichita I

took a second look. To learn more about the whole matter I attended an open-air meeting in a nearby community at which Vincent Harding, a Mennonite Negro
minister, related his experiences while traveling in the
Deep South. He was denied the use of rest rooms, or the
privilege of entering certain restaurants, hotels, and the
like. The report was well given, a straightforward account of actual conditions.

At the close of the service he taught the audience the
civil rights song, "We Shall Overcome." Slow, dirge-like,
we sang it but without the depth of feeling with which I
have heard it sung over television. I sensed a strange
restraint on the part of myself and others in that almost
completely white audience. The restraint seemed to say,
"Negroes should have civil rights, but must I, as a white
person, identify myself with them completely to help
them achieve their freedom?"

These are my basic attitudes at the moment, satisfac-
tory to myself to a point, and yet not completely satisfying. My daughter, a high school senior, said to me the
other day, "Mother, when I hear all about these social
problems in the world, I feel I'm not doing anything to
help the situation. I feel so useless. I sometimes think I
would like to join a civil rights demonstration." Is action
added to attitudes a more satisfying solution to an individual's personal struggle for answers to such social
needs?   —Written about 1965.

If, as you begin to list some of the events which had a
share in forming the attitude you wish to write about,
you feel uncomfortable about them, admit this to yourself and ask yourself why. I have ambivalent feelings
about my size. I always thought of myself as a fat child. I

would stand in front of a mirror sideways and suck in my stomach to see if I couldn't develop a waistline and be beautiful. But always my youthful appetite and Mother's excellent cooking overcame me. I'd fill up again on rolls stuffed with jam, or big plate-size pancakes covered with syrup—seven or eight of them. But even now, as I rush past store windows, another person reflected in the glass looks out at me, and it isn't a stout woman; but she haughtily greets the fat person in me.

One last bit of advice: To say something was meaningful does not make the event meaningful unless you show the reader the selected facts and details which made it meaningful. To say something was exciting ("The trip was exciting") or interesting ("The book was interesting") does not make it exciting or interesting to the reader. To say you like something ("The dress looked lovely") or that you thought something was a bad experience ("The trip was disappointing") does not tell the reader why you thought the dress was lovely or the trip was disappointing. Such words are like empty conduits—they carry little meaning, only an expression of your opinion. The reader does not know what you are responding to or what degree of liking or disappointment you are expressing. So instead of writing "I enjoyed Mother's meals," write: "I liked coming home to Mother's dinners each noon after trudging through the nippy winter air. I knew she would have a meal of cooked navy beans and sausage with onion cream gravy, or of mashed potatoes and big meatballs, waiting for us. Sometimes for dessert she prepared chocolate pudding, nearly frozen, with whipped cream—and always lots of everything."

Use simple, but natural sounding language to make

your writing meaningful. Don't write to impress. Write to express. Use specific, concrete words, instead of abstract, general ones. Abstract words refer to intangible qualities like love, hope, sorrow, comfort, sweetness. Concrete words stand for anything which can be pictured or specified, such as a tree, house, lake, or suitcase. If the reader can create an image in his or her own mind, your meaning moves out of your words more easily. Abstract words like honor, truth, and righteousness are hard to visualize, for they have broad meanings and can be interpreted in many ways. So when Christ spoke about love, He created an image by talking about a cup of cold water or visiting the imprisoned. Then His listeners knew what He was talking about, and there wasn't any of this nonsense about love never having to say you're sorry.

As you write, consciously prefer specific words to general words. General words refer to a broad class or category, such as dwellings, animals, humankind. I think of them as faraway words, the kinds of words you use when you can't see clearly what is before you. "I see something moving in the distance," you tell your friend. Then as that "thing" comes closer, you recognize it as being a person, then a man, then a young man in blue jeans, and by this time, as your brother Bob. "Bob" is specific, but "something" is vague and hard to visualize.

So, instead of writing, "There was something lying on the table," or "There was some food on the table," write, "There was a birthday cake with pink icing and candles on the table." Instead of writing, "My father was a generous man," write, "Though we were poor and my father had no job, when company came, he went to town to buy some bologna we could hardly afford, to feed our guests."

Meaningful writing is your goal at all times. A life is always more than a series of biological events such as birth, marriage, illness, death, and so forth. It is more than a series of rites of passage such as kindergarten, high school, first love, first car, first job, retirement. A memoir can become richer when you tell not only what you did, but also how you became the person you are. Blend the world of facts with the world of the inner life at each step.

CHAPTER SEVEN

A Special Kind of Wealth

Most families have at least one skeleton in the closet, like a jilted bride or a runaway son and heir, perhaps even a ghost or two, or something worse. My children, when younger, thrilled to read the notation after one name in our family genealogy which states, "She was reported to be a witch." To have a real witch in the family sounds more exciting than owning a miller or even a missionary.

The memory closets of all families hold another kind of wealth, more valuable than skeletons with flesh or without. These treasures include the family folklore— anecdotes, parables, proverbs, humor, jokes, games, festivals, customs, and stories about personalities and incidents in the family history which have human interest. Some have been discarded as trivial and others forgotten through neglect. Bring them back to life in your memoirs. They reveal much about your family.

Collecting family lore may take time, but will reward you in many ways—first, by the good times you will have digging for it with other family members; and second, by the mounds of little treasures you can share with your reader which will tell you both a little more about the quality of your family life.

You may insert such material in your writing wherever it is appropriate, or you may want to make a special chapter of it. To collect family folklore and customs, establish categories such as I have included in this chapter; and as you come across an item, write it on a half sheet of paper together with the source and date, and add it to your file. Then, later, use it as needed.

1. *Legends, Myths, Folktales, Parables, Ghost Stories, Endless Tales*

A well-known legend growing girls were reminded of in an earlier decade concerned a proud young woman who had had her hair done in a bouffant style at the hairdressers and refused to comb it thoroughly between settings. She died suddenly one day. The mortician found a black widow spider had made a nest in her fancy hairdo. She had died of an insect bite. We would suffer the same disaster if we didn't comb our hair thoroughly.

You have probably also heard of the man's body found in a manufacturer's pickle vat; sometimes it is a soft drink bottling company. Another common story was about the woman diner who asked the chef for the recipe of Red Velvet Cake served at the Hotel Waldorf. He sent it to her with a charge for $500. To spite him, she passed the recipe on to all her friends, and for a while the recipe appeared in many magazines and papers. Yet the hotel denies the story, according to folklore experts.

A few years ago the story was passed around that several men had picked up a hitchhiker on the West Coast. He told them the world would soon end and

Christ would return. They turned to speak to him, but he had disappeared from the car. No doors had been opened.

As children, we listened fearfully to ghost stories and stories about Satan, especially one about a young man who sold his soul to the devil. After the transaction, five strong men were needed to hold him down. He possessed such supernatural powers, he could literally climb the walls.

Another ghost story which made our blood run cold involved the daughter of a wealthy elder in the Mennonite church in Russia. Her father had occasion to have much contact with officials in the Russian government. So it happened that the daughter, a beautiful young woman, met and fell in love with a young man of Russian royal blood. But marriage to him was out of the question, for how could a member of the Russian nobility marry a commoner, and a German at that? The elder and his family also opposed the marriage for religious reasons.

But the young couple met secretly against their parents' wishes; so to stop further problems, the young woman was married off by her parents, against her will, to a nice young man in the village. He had no extremely objectionable qualities and no extremely commendable ones. In time, everyone forgot about the young man from the city who had once loved the young woman and been rejected because of his royal blood. Later, rumors moved through the community that he had committed suicide out of despondency, but no one was sure of the truth.

After several years of marriage the young woman became seriously ill and died. A young man was sent on horseback to relatives in distant villages to tell them the sad news. Because it was summer, the weather warm,

and the village without undertakers, her body was
bathed with alcohol to preserve it and laid out in the
cool, dark summer kitchen until the relatives would ar-
rive for the funeral.

After a day in mourning, the family came to the summer kitchen to pay their last respects to the dead woman
only to find she had come back to life. They found her
sitting up and asking for help to get down from the
boards on which she had been laid out for burial. She
said she was cold, so they quickly brought her into the
house, gave her hot coffee to drink, and wrapped her in
warmed blankets and hot water bottles. The woman
never again joked or smiled, nor would she talk about her
experience with death.

Eight years later her husband woke up one morning to
find his wife missing from their bed. He waited for her to
return, thinking she might have gone to the outdoor
privy. He waited, but she didn't return, so he got up to
look for her. The whole village was alerted to look for the
missing woman, but she couldn't be found.

That day the husband's cousin, who lived ten miles
downstream, decided to visit the village. On his arrival,
upon being told the sad news of the disappearance of the
woman, he recalled that two Russian fisherman had told
him they had seen a corpse lying along the river's edge.
So the husband and his cousin rowed down the river,
scanning the banks for the body. Perchance it might be
the missing woman. About four miles from home, they
found her, in her white nightgown, dead. Footprints
proved she had walked there by herself. So the body was
brought home and buried.

The night she disappeared, a neighbor had been up
very late. She heard dogs barking wildly and looked out

the window to see two persons in white walking outside. She called her husband to look, but by the time he came to the window, the figures had disappeared.

Another villager came home from fishing late the same evening. As he docked his boat he saw another boat on the river with two persons in white sitting in it. Both he and his wife saw the figures. They talked to them, but the figures remained mute. After a few moments, the boat and its occupants disappeared.

The day of the funeral the neighbor woman saw two persons in white moving across the garden as she milked the cow outside the barn. The cow shied at the sight of them. The same evening a brother-in-law of the dead woman was looking for some lost horses in the fields. As he rode past the cemetery with its freshly covered grave, his horse reared so that he could hardly control his mount. He looked up to see two persons in white standing by the new grave. Who could it be but the two persons separated in life because of their differing positions, but now united in death?

If, after hearing this story shortly before bedtime, I heard a dog barking wildly in the distance, you can well imagine I buried my head deeply under the covers.

I preferred to hear my sister tell one of her endless tales: One cold and stormy night seven robbers were in a cave. One robber said to another robber, "Antonio, tell us a tale." Antonio began as follows: "One cold and stormy night seven robbers were in a cave. One robber said to another robber, 'Antonio, tell us a tale.' Antonio began as follows: 'One cold and stormy night seven robbers were in a cave. One robber said to another. . . .' "

By that time we'd usually say, "Annie, go to sleep." And we all did.

2. *Epigrams, Proverbs, Witticisms*
   My parents often replied to the questions we children asked with proverbs, probably because their parents had done the same to them. A gentle kind of folk wisdom was passed on through these Low German sayings: If it tastes good, buy some for yourself too; Many guests make an empty pantry; A stitch in time saves nine; Limitations reveal the master-worker; Don't count your chickens before they're hatched; Sing before breakfast, cry before supper.
   If we asked too many pointed questions, the vague answer was followed by, "Children's questions sprinkled with sugar," or that the event we were expectantly awaiting would happen "next summer on Sunday three weeks later in the afternoon."

3. *Folk Songs, Hymns, Children's Prayers, Table Songs*
   Nearly every family has at least a few choice memories of heads bowed while tender voices rattled off a prayer in unison at the table. Perhaps you sang a song together.
   Did you say either of these prayers as children?

> Now I lay me down to sleep,
> I pray Thee, Lord, my soul to keep.
> If I should die before I wake
> I pray Thee, Lord, my soul to take.

> God is great, God is good,
> Let us thank Him for this food.
> By His hand we all are fed,
> Give us, Lord, our daily bread.

As a child I remember listening to people of the community singing "Prisoner's Song," "Hello, Central, Give

Me Heaven, for My Daddy's There," "The Drunkard's Daughter," and a few similar tear-jerkers at concerts. Among the popular cowboy songs were "Red River Valley," "Springtime in the Rockies," and "Home on the Range." Folk tunes included those we learned at school and at summer camp, such as "There's a Hole in the Bottom of the Sea," "Where, Oh Where Is Pretty Little Susie?" and numerous songs like "Three Blind Mice," "Row, Row, Row Your Boat," and "Are You Sleeping, Brother John?"

Some trite little ditties were used to make fun of people we didn't like:

> Here comes the bride,
> Big, fat, and wide.
> See how she wobbles
> From side to side.

If we saw love in bloom, we'd say:

> First comes love, then comes marriage,
> Then they come with a baby carriage.

Every family had a few songs sung to amuse children:

> This little pig went to market,
> This little pig stayed home,
> This little pig had roast beef,
> And this little pig had none,
> And this little pig went crying, "Wee, wee, wee,"
> All the way home.

We children grew up reciting nonsense rhymes in Low German because we loved the way the syllables rolled off our tongues and conveyed the right emotion:

Mi hungat, Mi schlungat, Mi schlackat de Buck.
(I'm hungry, so hungry, my belly is shaking.)

Schokel, schokel, scheia,
Ostre eet we Eia;
Pinkste eet we witet Brot;
Stoaw we nijh, dann woa we groot.

(Rock, rock, rock
Easter, we eat eggs;
Pentecost we eat white bread;
If we don't die, we'll grow up.)

Verses which incorporated wisdom and truth were inscribed in autograph books of friends, sometimes with ornate pen-and-ink drawing. True love was revealed by the amount of effort put into the penmanship and selection of the verse, but occasionally one had to resort to the less creative old favorites:

Some write for joy,
Some write for fame,
But I write only
To sign my name.

Don't be ♯
Don't be ♭
Just be ♮

2YS UR 2YS UB IC UR 2YS 4ME

Variations of well-known poems from literature classes were also used to meet autograph obligations, such as:

> Mary had a little lamb,
> Her father shot it dead;
> And now it goes to school with her
> Between two hunks of bread.
>
> Breathes there a man with soul so dead
> Who never to his wife has said,
> "Get over, and give me half the bed"?

If we wanted to be risqué, we would write:

> The boy stood on a burning deck,
> His feet were all in blisters.
> The flames crept up his pantlegs,
> And now he wears his sister's.

We also had rhymes for writing into books we loaned to friends:

> If by chance this book should roam,
> Box its ears and send it home.

And rhymes for reciting to ladybugs which accidentally settled on our clothing:

> Ladybug, ladybug, fly away home;
> Your house is on fire
> And your children are in it.

4. *Humor, Wit, Anecdotes, Jokes, Family Jokes*

Every family has special ways of using language for inside jokes which mean little to outsiders. Usually each family also has its store of tales about encounters with important personalities, children's misunderstandings of grown-up talk, as well as the odd tall tale or two.

My father hates to hurt the feelings of even a cat. Admonition or criticism must be slipped into conversation sideways, never directly. One day he stood at the street corner with the cane he uses in his old age and wearing heavy, dark glasses. Obviously he looked perplexed to the young woman who asked if she could help him cross the street. Dad agreed and let her guide him by the arm across the street, not wanting to embarrass her, and never letting on he wasn't blind and could make it on his own.

Dad liked to buy clothes for us girls at the local dry-goods store. Sometimes I think some of these purchases were used to offset debts in his store, so I'm not sure how the choices were made. One day he had bought Annie a dress, a nice dress, but it was too long, much too long. Mother decided it shouldn't be shortened. Annie would grow into it. Mother firmly believed children grew into anything, so clothes at first always tended to be a little on the long side. But Annie had to wear the dress to a school concert. She hated the folds of skirt flopping around her legs, so she ingeniously tucked the waistline into her belt in front, assuming the back didn't matter. Mother saw her from the audience and sent word down the chorus line for Annie to pull her skirt down all around. Annie complied and maintains to this day everyone thought she was singing in her nightgown.

No one smoked in our home. Yet one evening a local bachelor of what I thought was considerable age asked me if I would skate with him that evening at the local skating rink where we young people spent a good part of every evening. At the rink I donned my skates, and gracefully glided out onto the ice. The young (old) man saw me and dashed out for the promised skate. But he had been smoking, and stuffed his cigarette in his back pocket to save it for later. As we drifted around the rink to the strains of "The Beautiful Blue Danube," I became aware of other skaters shouting and pointing at us. I turned around. A thin line of smoke was issuing from my partner's back pocket. That relationship went up in smoke before it ever began. Once again, I'm sure my father was very happy; for though he had surely planned an ending, he would probably have tried a different one.

5. *Children's Games, Youth Activities, and Pastimes*

Every evening, all summer, we children played outside in the empty lot until finally it was too dark to see even the whites of our eyes. We had a repertoire of games which surpassed the number of toys a modern child owns. A large group could play Anthony Over (Auntie-I-Over), Flying Dutchman, Run My Good Sheep Run, Hide and Go Seek, It, Prisoner's Base, May I? London Bridge, Here We Go Round the Mulberry Bush, Red Rover, Two-Deep, Drop the Handkerchief, Tag, Fox and Geese (in the snow), Statue, Scrub, and softball. Most of these games had their special rituals, such as how to choose sides (hand over hand on the bat when playing ball, or spinning the racket when playing tennis, etc.).

If there weren't enough children available for a group game, two or three played marbles, jacks, knife, hop-scotch, teeter-totter, swing, or even work-up. Skipping rope was mostly a girls' game accompanied by rhymes about girls' activities to test our aerobic skills:

> I love coffee, I love tea,
> How many boys are stuck on me?
> One, two, three, four. . . .

At this line the ropeholders turned the rope at higher speeds until the girl tripped and was out. When we got tired of this one we chanted other rhymes:

> Grace, Grace, dressed in lace,
> Went upstairs to powder her face,
> How many boxes did she use?
> One, two, three, four. . . .
>
> Salt, vinegar, mustard, pepper. . . .

If the weather wasn't cooperative, in the parlor we played such games as forfeits, charades, spin the pie plate, blindman's bluff, pin the donkey, checkers, Monopoly, Parchesi, tiddly winks, pick-up sticks, or various kinds of pencil games such as tic-tac-toe, squares, hangman, and battleship.

A continual challenge to our imagination during preadolescence was to find out the name of our future husband by setting our name beside some boy's and crossing out all identical letters. Sometimes we added made-up second names, if we thought it might help. Or we plucked the petals from a flower while chanting, "He loves me, he loves me not." Other equally important pastimes were saving and trading hockey pictures, comic books, marbles, pieces of colored broken glass, and pretty pieces of cloth or ribbon. We could tell if a person loved butter by rubbing his or her throat with a dandelion, and we knew someone was talking about us if our own ears were ringing.

6. *Superstitions, Fetishes*

While the tooth fairy probably lived in many homes, most parents would not openly admit to being superstitious. Yet we children picked up more than our share of superstitious practices, which we clung to with the seriousness of death, and then as quickly dropped when we found new securities.

Walk under a ladder and bad luck will befall you.

Step on a crack and break your grandmother's back.

If a black cat crosses your path, you will have bad luck.

For a happy marriage, wear something old, something new, something borrowed, something blue.

Avoid the number 13.

Touch wood after boasting to avoid bad luck.

If you peel an apple in one piece and throw the peeling over your left shoulder, it will form the first letter of the name of the man you will marry. (We sometimes shoved it into the right shape.)

To break off the bigger end of the wishbone means your wish will come true.

If you count one hundred white horses, the first person you meet thereafter will be your husband. (Sometimes, as the supply of horses dwindled, it took us two summers to count one hundred!)

If you accidentally say the same words as someone else, you are required to clasp little fingers and say, "Needles, pins, my side wins."

Among the older folks, the superstitions related to

more adult activities. A pregnant woman was not allowed to use the telephone. If she was suddenly frightened, the baby would be marked and might even resemble an animal. A copper bracelet alleviated arthritis. A rabbit's foot brought good luck.

7. *Home Remedies for the Sick*

In the absence of doctors and nurses, and even hospitals, every mother had her supply of home remedies for all types of illnesses. When we had colds, we wore cloths rubbed with camphor applied to the throat and wrapped with woolen scarves. Many children came to school so attired. Wart remedies were as varied as the reasons one got warts. Every family had its method of stopping hiccoughs and sneezes.

Other home cures included fresh pig manure to stop bleeding (but not in our home), peppermint oil for colic, browned flour for diaper rash, goose grease for a cold, turpentine on a sugar cube, or honey in milk or in hot lemon tea, for a cough. Warm oil was applied for an inner-ear infection and cloves for a toothache. Hot compresses were used for boils, epsom salts or baking soda or vinegar for mosquito bites and other stings, hot saltwater to gargle for colds, kerosene to wash the hair for dandruff, and *Alpenkräuter,* a popular over-the-counter medicine (with 14 percent alcohol content) for what ails you.

In a slightly different category were concoctions to make girls more beautiful, such as lemon juice to brighten the hair, cooked flaxseed for hairsetting gel, and mashed cucumbers for a face mask. My sister tells me this hairsetting lotion was made by boiling together one-half cup of linseed with two cups of water. The mixture

was strained and cooled, then applied to the hair before
setting finger waves. It set hair like cement, she reports.
One day Frieda did Annie's hair with the linseed lotion
and produced a wave "as big as a hand." It probably
caused tears then, but much laughter now, as Anne
describes how she could put a whole hand into the
trough of this massive finger wave, fit to be entered in
Guinness Book of Records.

8. *Festivals and Celebrations*

The glue that held early families and communities
together were the many occasions they celebrated
together, such as a wedding, a family reunion, a picnic,
special days like Christmas, Easter, or Thanksgiving, or
religious observances such as christenings, baptisms,
communions, or even funerals.

Families have their own ways of making such times
special. At the birth of a baby some proud papas hand
out cigars; and if they don't smoke, it is candy bars. At
birthdays we used to pinch the child of honor and give
him or her a spank for each year. Fortunate children had
parties with gifts and wishes, and the blowing out of the
birthday cake candles. In some homes the birthday child
could plan the menu for one meal, even if it was all junk
food.

Courtship brought with it its share of rituals from bun-
dling and shivareeing of very early days to church sings,
blind dates, promise rings, engagement rings, showers
for the engaged girl, and stag parties in later years.

Some communities sponsored work parties to help
families out, coming together to quilt, thresh, can, or
build a barn or house. The younger set had taffy pulls,
bean suppers, and wiener roasts outside in some farmer's

field. Then they flopped onto a hayrack for the long, slow ride home under a harvest moon. Ice-cream socials, spelling bees, and teas were popular when I was a child. Each of the special days of the calendar had its prescribed activities, such as April Fool's Day, Valentine's Day, Mother's Day, Halloween.

As you write about these special celebrations, ask yourself, who organized and saw them through? Who came to them? How were they conducted? What values and traditions did they perpetuate? Why did they change or stop?

As you look for these special kinds of wealth to enrich your memoirs, don't forget early cooking experiences and some of the strange recipes so popular then. Include also early farm and business practices, such as hog butchering, waterwitching, harvesting, sheepshearing, marketing, auctioneering, and homecrafts such as carding and spinning wool, weaving, quilting, and sewing. You may also want to include something about the style of architecture, costumes, and music of the time when you were young.

A little more difficult to recall, but well worth the effort, is the inclusion of speech patterns and gestures peculiar to your family and locality. These might include regional variations in vocabulary, pronunciation, and word order, but also the slang of your youth. In my teen years we spoke nonchalantly of being "fit as a fiddle," and "snug as a bug in a rug." We said, "Phooey on you," "Oh, yeah," "Kiddo," and other daring things. We had nicknames for special friends, such as Spundoolicks and Honeybunch, and some for the not-so-special, which are best left out.

We developed a language of gestures to communicate

without words behind parents' backs, such as holding one's nose between thumb and forefinger while making a face, thumbing one's nose, sticking out one's tongue, rubbing one forefinger over the other while saying, "Shame, shame, double shame, everybody knows your name." Adults had their own supply of gestures, such as a hearty handshake, the victory sign, shaking a forefinger vigorously at a child offender. Men sometimes kissed men and women kissed women, but men seldom kissed women in the presence of children; so love scenes in movies and dramas were looked at rapturously, with the knowledge they represented dangerous temptations.

Once you begin digging for this kind of treasure in your past, you will find the supply almost limitless. Every person has a huge supply of folklore for the asking.

CHAPTER EIGHT

If You Hit a Few Snags

By now you will have spent many hours writing and also many hours thinking and wondering where this new project is leading you. What you started to do may now be directing you and taking on a shape and will of its own, letting you know what needs to be written. Doubtless you have also run across a few snags.

1. *What do I do about stories that contain unpleasant elements?*

Some stories will be hard to write about because they may embarrass or cause hard feelings in the family or community. Some memories may be so poignantly bitter or sweet, you don't want the whole world to know about them. Should you include them?

Your material is always your own, and you are free to select what you want to include in your memoirs. You are never obligated to tell all and turn your manuscript into a racy true confession. If you are dealing with difficult incidents such as attempted suicide, abortion, alcoholism, child abuse, unfaithfulness, incessant fighting in the home, criminal acts, misuse of authority, or other types of difficult behavior, you may wonder whether it is necessary to explain what happened and to whom. Obviously, you can't make a disclaimer at the beginning of your memoirs that all characters in it are fictional.

Ask yourself if your story will hurt anyone if you bring it into the open. Was it common knowledge at the time it happened? Did it affect a large group of people then, or were only a few people aware of it? Does it deliberately vilify? Does your telling of it show malice or spite? Is it necessary to the rest of your story? Is it fair to all concerned? Will it build good will and better friendships, which you value, or will it destroy them? Are you telling this story only for its sensational value?

Are the people involved still alive? Can you talk to them about it? How will it affect any children who are involved? Will you be open to a libel suit if you publish this material? What will be gained if you include it? How important is it to your story? What will be lost if you omit it from your story?

A small piece of advice I find helpful is never to exploit deliberately your children's involvement in your life to show readers how you see truth. They will have to live with whatever you write about them. Let the children do their own telling. Never misuse other people's experiences or confidences to sensationalize your writing either. In this book I have deliberately left out the rough times when it seemed our usual family solidarity wouldn't survive the pressures of social change, the war, and the growing pains of a family of teenagers. At a later date, after I have discussed these experiences with my brother and sisters, I may be able to include them in a public writing.

2. *What do I do if I can't remember?*

Leave out the section where your memory refuses to cooperate, and work on other parts for a while. Sometimes you will find that while you were occupied with these other chapters, your subconscious mind was working for you and has surfaced the details you thought you had forgotten. If this approach doesn't work and you can't locate more information about the story, leave it out. Don't force a story where there is none. If you've come to a dead end, admit it and move on. You can't tell everything, not even all you consciously remember. Writing is always a matter of choosing facts, ideas, incidents, impressions to meet your thematic purpose. You will also soon realize you find it easier to remember what happened in early childhood than in the immediate past.

3. *How do I handle victories and successes without appearing boastful, and moments of despair and defeat without seeming to look for pity?*

V. S. Pritchett in "Writing an Autobiography" (edited by Francis Brown, New York: Holt, Rinehart & Winston, Inc., 1969) says the three main difficulties in writing about one's own life are self-pity, a sense of shame, and self-justification. Boasting may be another, though he doesn't mention it. It is difficult to record the opinions one held at an earlier time truthfully, Pritchett says, for in later years, one forgets how strong they once were. In the meantime, these opinions have changed because of circumstances.

As you write your memoirs, you will find self-pity the easiest of the three dangers Pritchett mentions to spot in your own material.

When you sense the tone becoming whiny and pity-seeking, use your blue pencil freely. By carefully watching your words, you can avoid wallowing in shame over past failures or boasting too loudly of past prowess. Deal with such events objectively, dwelling on the facts of the event, rather than on your shame or pride.

In writing about heroic and embarrassing incidents, emphasize the event itself and the truth of the event. This will help you control your writing and make the incident a natural part of your past, instead of sounding like bragging or apologizing.

The real problem in autobiographical writing, according to Pritchett, is how to avoid subtle and secretive self-justification, especially when you are recording emotions and beliefs you once held, but which you have long since discarded.

Maybe once you were a full-throated hawk; now you are a clear-voiced dove. The record in written word and in the memory of colleagues clearly shows you once advocated the use of violence and aggression in national conflicts. But now you are living in a present totally unlike the past when your hawk-like attitudes thrived. You wonder: Did I actually write strong letters to the editor of the local paper about the Vietnamese draft-dodgers? Deliberately reckon on the power of your present attitudes to deceive yourself about how strong those old attitudes were when you held them.

As you write, you will find yourself desperately wanting to show that the position you held in the past did not have a lasting effect, or at least was justified at the time. It is extremely difficult to be honest about past convictions about any serious issue, including your commitment to God's will. Most of us find it hard to acknowledge that even while we clung to high-sounding ambitions to serve God and our fellow human beings in the vocation we chose, we also secretly cherished opportunities to gratify self-interests.

Where you are now in terms of age, wealth, position, friends, and theology will influence how you view the past. If you are content now, though the past may have included many difficulties (such as having to drop out of school early, living with an alcoholic father, being forced to support yourself through school), you will probably see the past with a measure of acceptance. Those things were part of your past, but you survived them. If you are unhappy now, you may tend to blame the past, and especially parents, teachers, church and civic leaders, for your present situation. Occasionally, older persons are eager to write about their previous experiences for only one reason: so that their slant on events will not be lost and that everyone will know that "at that point we got a dirty deal from the government (or from other kinds of leaders)."

4. *Are there any particular dangers for the writer of a minority group?*

Merle Good in "Exploitation and Storytelling" in *Festival Quarterly* (Winter 1975) points to two dangers for the storyteller from a minority group. The first is to lecture one's own people on their inadequacies and backwardness while seeking to usher them into the "modern" era. The assumption here is that the old subculture must be improved and thereby destroyed. What's modern is better, if for no other reason than comfort and acceptability. The memoir writer of a minority group may likewise be tempted to lecture the reader about the inadequacies of his or her particular past instead of owning it and thereby being freed of it.

Good states a second danger for the minority writers is to protect their world at all costs, with the result that they write "romantically and defensively" about their people without an honest appraisal of the contrast between their ideals and their practices. "The theme 'we can't wash our dirty linens in public' becomes a hymn of dishonesty to keep us from admitting the truth about ourselves," says Good. In biographical writing the first danger (being too critical) is termed debunking, and the second (being too generous), hagiography, or idealizing the person being written about. The better way is to choose a middle road. Strike a balance between painting your verbal pictures all black or all white. A good photograph includes many shades in between, and the result can still be a prize-winning photo.

5. *How do I begin the process of review and revision?*

Before you start revising, review again some of the characteristics of good autobiographical writing:

—It is always individualized. It is the interpretation of your life according to your understanding. It will reveal the peculiarities of your life and those qualities and acts that make you different from other people, as well as those you have in common with them. It will be your story, no one else's.

—It is always true, in the sense that you do not create events, characters, or dates. The characters the novelist invents may be unusual and vivid and seem true to life, but they cannot equal the fascination of persons who really lived. Your memoirs should be true and truth-seeking.

—The aim of such memoirs is to entertain, to inform,

to offer yourself as an example of the human process. You are concerned with shaping, with making sense out of the past from the standpoint of a present that is quite different. Therefore your memoirs will never be the whole story, only a part of it.

Go over your manuscript carefully several times, as if it belonged to a stranger. Read it with a sense of detachment. Take another look at form, order, clarity of ideas. Double-check all names, dates, and statements of fact. Have someone else read it for grammar, spelling, punctuation, sentence structure, consistency of style, and wordiness. Be sure you retain a carbon copy of your writing, so that if the original is lost, you have a copy in your possession.

6. *How do I go about getting it published?*

This question is answered by the audience you have written your memoirs for, the size of that audience, and sometimes the funds available to you for publication. You have several options open to you.

—Have some capable person type your manuscript on a typewriter with carbon ribbon, and then have it duplicated by a commercial duplicating service if you need only a few copies for family members. You might also consider mimeograph, but for clear permanent copies stay away from carbon paper reproduction and spirit duplicating. You can purchase substantial binders in any large office supply store to provide an attractive and durable setting for your material.

—Royalty publisher. Such publishers are usually not interested in private memoirs unless they are written by someone of national importance in some particular field (politics, religion, education, and the like) and the publisher can be assured of a large reading audience. Under such an arrangement, the publisher assumes full responsibility for editing, publishing, and distributing your material, and pays the author a stipulated royalty. If your material has little significance beyond the immediate family, you may find a better solution in one of the other options.

—Private printing by a commercial printing press. When you select a commercial printing press to print your material, you become the publisher of your own book and bear all costs of editing, cover design, format, advertising, shipping, and distribution. Some writers take this route because then they don't have to wait for a publisher's acceptance of their manuscript. They make the decision whether they want it published.

—Subsidy (vanity publishing). This type of publishing differs from private publishing in that the vanity publisher offers some fringe benefits such as editing, text and cover design, warehousing, advertising, and distribution for a fee for such professional services. The expense of publishing is borne completely by the author, and ownership of the material is retained by the author. Vanity publishers, however, have bad names in literary circles. There have been some exceptions, but, in general, fairly or not, reviewers tend to toss the books of vanity publishers aside and libraries do not acquire them for their holdings. Vanity publishers have a reputation for being exploitive in that they praise manuscripts beyond their true worth, so that new writers are led to believe they have a product which will make them rich. If you publish your manuscript yourself, you can order as few copies as you need. With a vanity publisher, you are pushed to buy more than you will need. Further, the promises of such publishers to advertise and promote your book do not always hold up.

So, you may do best if you follow the example of the elderly woman who had completed her memoirs. A subsidy publisher offered to publish them for $4,000. Her friends advised her not to do so but wait until a royalty publisher accepted them. Her answer to them was, "I'm 83, you know. I've been through the Victorian era. I want to leave a book behind but the publishers say they have hundreds of 'that type.' " She added that publishers she had contacted took six months to reply to her letters. "That's fine if you live to be 150." She published her memoirs herself. I recommend you go and do likewise.

7. *What about obtaining a copyright?*

Under the new Copyright Law effective January 1, 1978, a manuscript can be copyrighted before publication. Previously a manuscript was protected under common law before publication. For your protection against plagiarism your finished work should be registered for copyright protection regardless whether it is published or remains unpublished. The duration of the copyright is the author's life plus fifty years. Under the old copyright law, a copyright was good for 28 years and could be renewed for another 28.

If you do not copyright a work and only a relatively small number of copies are distributed, your work is still eligible for protection for at least five years after publication if steps are taken to correct the error within this time. This includes registering the work, making a reasonable effort to put the correct notice on copies already distributed (© All Rights Reserved), and putting the correct notice on all other copies to be distributed.

Your book should be registered with the Library of Congress in Washington (or the Library of Parliament in Ottawa for Canadians). In each case the library files two copies with a number for cataloging purposes. To have your book registered, send two copies to the national library, where they become part of the permanent book collection of the country. Forms for filing for copyright and library registration, with details regarding fees, are available from Register of Copyrights, Copyright Office, Library of Congress, Washington, D.C. 20559.

You should also consider placing a copy of your memoirs with your local community library and your historical library.

Whatever method of publishing you choose, you will have to decide whether to include photos, charts, drawings, and so forth. By now you will also have chosen a title for the entire manuscript and for each chapter. And by now you may also have become a little weary of your project. But the rewards are still ahead.

Some people get hung up on politics or stamp collecting. I've got this thing about biography and memoirs. I admit to it readily. I'm always telling older people to write down their experiences—if not for their own benefit, then for a future biographer or for the historical society, or simply for their children.

Not all people understand why. Why immortalize in print the many little events which make up a person's life? Clyde S. Kilby writes in *Christianity and Aesthetics:* "Man is a creature of memory and uses memory not alone to know where he has been, but also to instruct him in where he is going. ... Man has a deep-seated desire for unity of being." This unity of being is expressed in your memoirs. When you present someone dear to you with a copy of your writing, you have given them a written picture of how you see the world and how this viewing has freed you to move on. And their thanks won't be long in coming. My children have already thanked me for the following story and are asking for more.

In it I deal with an aspect of my heritage which was a problem to me for many years. This piece could be lengthened in numerous places, but it will show you how you could handle some of the vague feelings of discomfort you may have had about your childhood. Notice how I have incorporated some of the information included in earlier chapters.

You Never Gave Me a Name

One day at school some snot-nosed English child informed me I was a Mennonite. To us children, anyone who was not born of immigrant parents was English, even if the person was anything else, like Irish or French. It had to have been an English kid, for they thought of themselves as being on top of the heap. I think I was about ten or eleven. At noon I rushed home the three long blocks, taking the back alley shortcut behind Batanoffs' house and through the gap between Swystun's tailor shop and Koval's shoemaker shop to make it to our wooden gate in record time. Once inside the door, I asked Mother the question on my mind.

Ja, Kind, wir sind Mennoniten.

She had never withheld this information from us children. I knew that. And I had known what her answer would be. But to be told this by an outsider seemed so final—almost as final as the eternal hellfire the preacher shouted about at the revival meetings in summer. Final and fatal. Now I was a Mennonite, whatever that meant.

I ate the dinner Mother had prepared for us. Mother was always at home waiting for her family to come to her from the outside. She seldom went shopping or visiting or to clubs or things like that. Mother was the home person, and always she had a meal waiting. Over the meal we told her what we had been doing that day in school. Mother worked at home cooking, cleaning, sewing, and mending. Mother worked and waited. I thought all mothers did only that.

I went back after dinner to the two-story red-brick schoolhouse at the far edge of the village. The cold October wind whipped around my brown lisle stockings and short coat. I dug my head deeper into its collar, not knowing quite what to do with this new knowledge.

For a few weeks the matter stayed uppermost in my mind. We were Mennonites, yet my parents spoke Russian as well as German. They had come to Canada in 1923 from the steppes of the Ukraine. Why weren't we Russians then, like the Nesdolys; or Ukrainian, like the Slywkas, who had also come from the same area? Somehow it didn't seem right to say we were German, or even Dutch. We were Russian Mennonites. Was that a religion, a nationality, or both—or neither?

My name was Katie, like that of any Russian girl—only she could call herself Katya, which sounded a little more cosmopolitan, I thought. My name was Katie, and my sisters were Annie and Frieda and Susie, and my brother was Jakie—plain Mennonite names.

But then, as the snow covered the streets and winter closed in, life resumed its normal course in this little village in northern Saskatchewan composed of many nationalities and creeds: Russian, Doukhobor, English, Scottish, Irish, French, Ukrainian, Polish, German,

Jewish, and some I have forgotten. Each morning at 7:30, Dad put on his white apron and left for the grocery store he managed in this farming community, to open it and get ready for the early morning trade: bread for breakfast, pencils for school, bologna for lunches. He set out the vegetables, brought up the farm produce from the basement, stoked the furnace in winter, cleaned out the ashes, and made grocery orders for the truck driver to take to the city, sixty miles distant.

We children grew into our turn to help in the store. My turn came after Frieda and Annie and before Susie and Jakie, at the tail end of the depression and during the early war years when business was done mostly with relief vouchers and credit. Farmers sometimes charged grocery bills for a whole year until they sold their harvest in fall. Then they walked in with a big roll of bills and said, "Jake, how much is it?" Dad would bring out a fistful of charge slips, add them up on the little adding machine, deduct a discount for some reason or other, and the farmer would hand over the right amount. There'd be a lot of good feeling passed around. And the next week the farmer would be back charging groceries again. And the farmer who couldn't pay sometimes took his trade to another store and left Dad with the stack of unpaid bills.

Most of the years I worked in the store a big copper cent bought one or two good-sized pieces of candy, and a nickel a chocolate bar or an ice-cream cone. Even a bottle of pop. Groceries were delivered to the well-to-do ladies of the community after they had either phoned in their order or walked daintily to the store and conveyed it to Dad. Then my brother or someone else delivered the groceries on a bicycle or pulled them to the home on a small wagon. Delivery was a free service to residents in town.

Groceries were never piled into sacks for those customers who wanted to carry them home, but packaged in paper, whether few or many. Dad taught me how to wrap big piles of assorted cans, boxes, and bags so that the package wouldn't fall apart in the bearer's arms on the way home. I learned to tie the package well, wrapping the string around my finger and giving it a quick jerk. Sometimes, if I didn't watch it, I developed a deep gouge in my finger from the sharp string. After a while I learned to protect my finger with a brown paper tape bandage each Saturday.

Dad also showed me how to make change, to fill shelves, to cut ten-cent wedges of cheese to order. Few customers were willing to pay for a twelve-cent piece of cheese, because it meant they had two cents less for something else then. I learned to weigh peanut butter into jars customers brought with them and to detect if the butter brought in by farm women for sale was rancid. Some of the lady customers opened each pound and nicked a little piece with a fingernail so they could taste it. We always told them who had made the butter, if we remembered; and so some women's homemade butter was more in demand than others. In fact, we saved it for favored customers.

Saturday nights the store stayed open until activity in town closed down. In summer, this sometimes took until well after midnight. When the dance in the Palace Theatre ended, the customers returned to the store to pick up their groceries (purchased earlier) now standing against the wall with their name and the words "Paid" or "Not Paid" crayoned on the box. Some bought additional groceries, depending, I guess, on how much money they had left after the dance and time spent in the pool hall. Dad, the clerk, and I rushed around bringing customers what they wanted—soap, salmon, bread, sugar, and hundred-pound bags of flour carried on Dad's shoulder. Then, finally, the last person was gone. At about 12:30 a.m. the cuckoo clock on the chimney wall crowed the time loud enough for me to hear. Sometimes it was closer to one o'clock. Dad would pull down the green wrinkled blind on the front door, pull his keys from his pocket and lock the door, and switch out some lights.

Nearly always Dad turned to me at this point, somewhat hesitatingly, brushing his forehead with that sweep of his hand that became more familiar over the years, and said, "Take a drink, Katie." He always said my name. I'd walk slowly to the open water cooler where the bottles were kept, and reach in, feeling in the dark water for a cold Orange Crush that had escaped someone else's search. I'd open it against the bottle opener on the side of the stand, letting the cap fall into the nearly full container (while reminding myself to empty it), and then I'd lean against the counter to drink and watch Dad. A soft drink. Once a week. My sisters and brothers didn't get one. My feet ached.

Dad and the clerk moved around quickly putting away perishables. Some were carried to the cooler basement. Those that remained on the display shelves were covered with a cloth so that the fly spray Dad waved around jerkily wouldn't fall on them. Then Dad'd hide the day's receipts, for the bank was closed. I wasn't supposed to be watching, but sometimes I knew he placed the little wooden box behind the soap boxes on the shelves, some-

times behind the coffee. Tonight he hid it in the cub-
byhole under the front-window display shelf. I knew
about that hole, but I never said anything.

"Go home, Katie." He'd let me out the door as soon as
I had finished my soft drink. I'd dash half a block home,
take a quick trip through the darkness to the outhouse
near the alley, ducking around the shadows of the bath-
house standing beside it. If it was very dark outside, or
the weather unfavorable, the garden served as well. And
then through the dark house upstairs to bed, where I
knew Mother would be lying waiting in the double bed
which nearly filled my parents' small bedroom.

"*Bist du das?* Katie?" Mother spoke German; we spoke
English. I'd whisper a brief "Dad's coming," and crawl
into bed beside Annie, hoping she wouldn't notice if I
pushed my cold feet gently against hers.

Our community was not overly religious, but a few
churches stood as sentinels at the corners of the town,
keeping sin and evil at bay. We children all witnessed
brawling fistfights on Main Street and were aware of un-
dercover bootlegging as close as next door. A Roman
Catholic church, with a fairly large parish and a 7:30
a.m. bell calling its parishioners to early Mass, protected
one side. Many of my schoolmates attended there, and
we always knew if it was Friday or Lent because they
couldn't eat meat. If we had a school party on a Friday,
they waited until midnight to eat, so they could enjoy the
meat sandwiches. Otherwise they ate egg or salmon
sandwiches. The United Church of Canada had a good-
sized Sunday school, a meager attendance at other
services, and a dwindling Ladies Aid that bought kitchen
ranges and curtains for the parsonage. This church could
be found if one poked through the bushes at the end of

the next street. An Anglican church, in which a visiting minister held services once a month, pointed its lonely spire to the sky at the far edge of town. That church was almost empty, it seemed. A Russian Baptist church in the country, with exuberant singing and lots of food on festival occasions, completed the church roster if we didn't count the Doukhobor Hall.

Christianity and churchgoing were important to my family. I soon realized that. Mother read us Bible stories and prayed with us every morning before we left for school. Dad was usually gone by the time we got up. The book she read from now stands on my bookshelf, and it barely holds together, so often did we page through it. Since churchgoing was needed for respectable living and personal integrity, and since our own church was not represented in this community, we lived a double life. In summer we were Mennonite Brethren and attended services in the small white frame building across the river about 20 miles away, sometimes feeling like worldlings prepared for the slaughter of the evangelist when we were dropped into that tight-knit Mennonite community. We always traveled to church by car semi-ready—our sashes for our dresses neatly folded in a long box, and our hair sometimes in rags. Before we walked into the church, Mother tied each sash into a big bow, combed our ringlets and adjusted our hair ribbons, and Dad gave us each a nickel. That was for the offering. There were two entrances side by side in this little white-frame church, one for women and one for men. The women sat on one side of the church and the men on the other. There was also a choir and, in later years, a piano and a children's picnic once a year, a *Kinderfest*, when the children got to eat first.

Sometimes my father preached; sometimes the red-necked farmers who had been working in the fields all week expounded the Word of God. Sometimes we brought along a picnic lunch; other times we were invited out for dinner. Sometimes we decided in the morning before we left whom we would visit that day, and we children always voted for a farm family so that we might get a chance to ride to church in the evening in a buggy or Bennett wagon (a horse-drawn, rubber-tired box wagon).

Coming home late in the evening after the Christian Endeavor program (we always stayed for C.E.) or a revival service, three children slumped together in the back seat of the 1925 McLaughlin-Buick bought from Dad's employer at a discount. It was a good buy, we knew. Buicks and Funks didn't really match. Another child hunched on an improvised jump seat and one squeezed between my parents while the car jerked homeward through the darkness on the rutty roads. Mother always held the door handle of the rear left door with one hand and a child with the other. Sometimes Dad would sing *Heimatlieder* (songs about heaven) brought along from Russia, where the war-weary Mennonites had found comfort in an other-worldliness once again. But then, as it grew darker, we children slept, borrowing a shoulder to lean on. We felt secure. Mom and Dad were in the front seat taking care of everything. It might be raining, the road slippery, and the ferry over the river not operating, but Dad and Mother would look after us.

But then in winter when the river froze over and the car was put on blocks, all our Mennonite friends were forgotten for seven to eight months. We children switched to being United Church, and Mother and Dad became Russian Baptists. Skating, Santa Claus, CGIT, bake sales, minstrel shows, amateur hours, Little Theater—these were now our activities. In the evenings in winter, when the nails in the siding of the house popped with the cold, my sister and I were sent as official representatives of the family to the evening service at the United Church while Dad toasted his feet in front of our pot-bellied stove. In later years, the Russian Baptist church moved into our house for Sunday services during the winter. The benches piled alongside the house were dusted free of snow, covered with blankets, and lined up in the living room.

Something came through to me slowly during these years. Being a Christian was important and somehow wasn't exactly connected with being a Mennonite. Those were two things—separate, yet at times one. Churchgoing was also important, but ecclesiastical hierarchies and any form of discrimination was taboo. Dad paid distant homage to institutions, and we children enjoyed our ecclesiastical freedom. I think we were glad. But switching from one brand of theology to another as the seasons changed complicated my thinking as I grew up.

For a long time we were the only Mennonites in the community, and I had all but forgotten what the little girl had told me that day in school. But periodically we were reminded of our heritage. In winter and summer our home was the official portage for all kinds of Mennonites, mostly poor, officially related to the church or unofficially detached from it. We children never knew when we would be transferred to a comforter on the floor in winter or to the playhouse behind the garage in summer to make room for a group of vacation Bible school workers or a homesteading family from the North, hungry for knowledge of relatives on the other side of the North Saskatchewan River. Hospitality was important to my parents until the winter when our guests brought bedbugs with them. Then, for a while, only a little while, their warmth cooled a little.

During these years I learned that though simple charity and honesty may not make a person rich, they help to preserve one's integrity. I heard often that Jake was the man who could be trusted to hold a paycheck so that the owner wouldn't spend it on drink; that he was a man of concern and kindness. It didn't matter to him if a customer used an X to sign his name. He filled out many forms and wrote many letters for townspeople who couldn't read or write. He identified with the Russians sometimes more than with the Mennonites, I thought, but his generosity extended to anyone in need.

I will never know how many boxes of groceries he gave away to Mother Hubbards and Popoffs and Kutnikoffs. I know only how many he delivered uncharged to my kitchen when my husband and I struggled on a low allowance while teaching, and later while studying. The cans were dented, and he couldn't sell them, he said; but we children joked that he threw them around so he would have something legitimate to give. My sister Annie recalls seeing him unobtrusively hand out loaves of bread and rings of sausage to hoboes on the way home from the store during the depression. The leader of the group tore at the sausage, breaking off chunks and handing them to the others. At times Dad would send a transient home to chop wood in exchange for a meal. Mother would bring everything she could find in her pantry to satisfy the man's hunger. Mother always treated each depression derelict like a guest, and that year our pile of split wood was larger than ever before. Annie says she received her first sense that people were hungry, perhaps starving, when the hoboes grabbed the food from Dad's hands or ate at our table.

After several years of our living in Blaine Lake as the only Mennonites, one day another Mennonite family moved to town. Mother and Dad now had some new friends. Then this family left, but soon another Mennonite family came. Again Mother and Dad had special friends who understood what lay behind the word "Mennonite." Not that they didn't have friends in town before this. Dad was on the village council of the community for nine years—an elected position—and Mother had teachers and ladies in for tea, and other women who came to talk. But these new ones were different because they knew what Mother and Dad had lived through in Russia, which created ties stronger than cracker barrel chatter. And with their coming came again the almost subconscious realization that we Funks were different. We weren't English, but we weren't Galicians or Doukhobors either, even though the latter were also conscientious objectors to war. We were poor, and so were our neighbors. But we were not their kind of poor. We never went on welfare regardless how tight the money situation became. And sometimes it was grim. Our current debts were listed on a piece of cardboard hung on the kitchen wall, and the day when Dad deducted his weekly pay from the total, the air was heavy. We were spending too much, yet we never saw a penny in cash. I couldn't always quite understand this. Mother made clothes for us girls out of Dad's old pants and shirts; and underwear, sheets, tea towels, and tablecloths from flour and sugar sacks. We wrapped our poverty in our moral integrity and struggled day by day. Dad didn't smoke or drink, and we children weren't allowed near the pool hall, not even for a quick look inside its murky darkness; but the Mennonite mystique was slowly making its mark on me—my roots were reaching out and claiming me, and I didn't know it.

In the evenings after Dad had come home from the store, and the dishes had been done, we all gathered around the round oak dining table with the woven covering, under the gas lamp in the little middle room. Dad worked at his accounts and orders for the store; Mother bent over her mending and knitting or helped the younger children with their reading. Each year Mother read through our readers so that she would learn to speak the language of this new country. We children did our homework or read or listened to the radio. Fibber McGee and Molly was a favorite show, as was Lux Theatre (but it got turned off quickly when the characters became too explicit in their relationship or language). And then, sometimes, during the evening hours the storytelling began. The stories Dad and Mother told were about another land in another time when they were young— and Dad would look at Mother in a special way I liked. Only many years later did I first see a picture of Mother as a young unmarried woman and found myself overcome by the clear-eyed beauty of her eyes and the regularity of her features.

I thought the stories my parents told were about a time at least a hundred years ago, perhaps even more. Only later, when I grew up, did I learn they had been telling us about what had happened only a decade or so ago. They talked about life as Mennonites on the steppes of the Ukraine, where their forefathers had fled to from

Prussia in search of religious freedom—freedom Catherine the Great had promised them. The Mennonite villages had prospered as a whole. Some people had become very rich; others remained very poor. Dad's relatives were always poor because they were landless. Mennonites were frugal, hard-working, honest people. They were true to God and to their calling as farmers. But World War I came. Young men were taken from the villages to serve as noncombatant medics in the army. Dad was one of these.

With the overthrow of the Tsarist government by the Bolsheviks in 1917, the revolution burst upon the entire nation. Total anarchy reigned for a while. Meanwhile the front of the Red and White armies in the revolutionary war shifted back and forth through the Ukraine, the site of the Mennonite colonies. "We had a cannon in our backyard," said Mother. That sentence told the whole story.

Fear and anxiety took on a new face when a large horde of bandits led by Nestor Makhno began plundering, murdering, and raping in the fall of 1919. I knew the horror of Makhno's name just about as soon as I could read. He and his men confiscated horses, furs, wagons, blankets, shoes, and food. They hacked people to death at whim. Victims in one Mennonite district totaled several hundred. I remember staring at pictures of the mass graves covered with a few flowers and surrounded by sad-faced mourners. Inside me was a heaviness I couldn't lift. All of Mother's trousseau was stolen during the revolutionary times. The wedding had been celebrated simply. A friend had buried some cabbage earlier, so it wouldn't be confiscated. It was dug up to make some *Borscht* for the wedding dinner, and to

Mother's embarrassment, the *Borscht* was served luke-
warm because someone forgot to keep the stove going.
Mother's parents didn't attend the wedding because they
had been lost in the confusion of the war. Dad agreed to
try to locate them when times became more settled.

Like the plagues of Egypt, the end of one siege meant
only the beginning of another. A new enemy moved in.
Hunger stepped into their midst and stayed, Mother told
us. In the spring of 1921 the last of the grain in some of
the Mennonite settlements was used up. Bread prices
and taxes rose. New taxes were introduced almost daily,
perhaps for each window in the house, each tree in the
orchard, or each son or daughter. Without money, the
people could not buy bread, nor was there much bread to
buy. My oldest sister, then a toddler, lost the ability to
walk because of poor nutrition. Mother and Dad's wedding rings were sold for food. Neither ever wore one
again, even after they could afford rings in Canada.
Rings are not needed to make a marriage, when it has
survived the violence and chaos of revolution, famine,
and emigration. The famine drove families to eat
whatever they could find. "We ate gophers and crows,"
said Dad. Bread was baked with anything that might
yield some nourishment, such as roots, leaves, corncobs,
or weeds.

People became sick with typhus during this period.
The aged, sick, and young children were affected most
by this disease. Each week the dead had to be disposed of
in ground hard with frost. Men weakened by long
months of hunger struggled to dig graves. Over a short
period of time, Dad, as the oldest male at home, prepared the bodies of his father, grandparents, and an
uncle for burial. Neighbors were too occupied with their

own sorrows to help him. He gave a laborer a pail of wheat to dig a grave shaped like an upside-down T. He built coffins with slats from the fence and put all four coffins in one grave, three in the first layer, and one on top. In spring, to his dismay, the grave had sunk into itself. He added a little dirt, not enough to level the ground, but it was all he could do.

Then one wonderful day, the word arrived that the Mennonites in the United States and Canada had heard of the plight of their brothers and sisters in the faith (or was it in the blood?) and were sending help. An American Mennonite Relief Administration Committee had been organized and an appeal sent to all American Mennonites for relief for the Russian Mennonites. Carloads of flour, other foodstuffs, and clothing were being sent to the Ukraine. Food kitchens were set up at various points to cook and distribute the food. Mother and Dad applied to work in one of these kitchens and were accepted. Mother was a good cook. In exchange for their work, they received rations for themselves and their two children. Mother's eyes still light up when she recalls the wonderfully soft buns the cooks baked with white flour that first time.

Night after night, year after year, in our frame wooden home in Blaine Lake, the stories of the Old Country were told. Never in an orderly manner. Little details were released at various times, like at a family gathering when suddenly an uncle or aunt began to reminisce about Russia, or while drying dishes, or when the mail brought a letter from relatives in Russia. Our Canadian relatives, including the jolly old grandmother in her long black dress and white apron, and some aunts, uncles, and cousins, all lived across the river. But there were still many relatives in Russia who showed up in the form of thin letters with writing that looked like straight lines joined with more straight lines, and covering every square centimeter of the thin paper, back and front. Gothic script, Mother called it. We tried to learn this script one summer, but I soon gave up.

The letters told about strange things happening in Russia, and about times getting harder, and about people—particularly men who were preachers and leaders—disappearing. One day I remember seeing my beautiful little mother with the auburn hair crying as she ironed clothes. A letter edged in black lay on the oilcloth-covered table. Her mother had died. Mother's mother had died. And she couldn't go back. The lady who died was not my grandmother; at least I never thought of her as such. Now the letter had come bringing the sad news. Mothers have mothers also, I learned, and people die. And families can't always be together when such things happen. It was another forceful link in the chain pulling me toward my past.

And then in the thirties for a long time no letters arrived, and the past which was Russia was left behind, even the ghost stories which we enjoyed so much. And we lived only in the present—this dual world—the world of Blaine Lake and school and skating and tennis and wiener roasts and young men going off to war; and that other world across the river of *Faspa* and riverside baptisms, horse-drawn buggies, and kneeling for prayer, and common cups, *Luther Übersetztung*, revival meetings, church discipline, Golden Texts, green curtains for class dividers, and audible prayer. Both were part of my experience, as well as the all-day mission festivals and family weddings in tents, and the head coverings and

silence and obedience for women. Yes, that silent waiting, too, was part of my life. And the kiss of peace and
conscientious objection to war.

But there was another world no one knew about. It was
my own world. Twilight became for me that precious
time to spend alone outside for a few last moments
before Mother called us in for the night to wash and go to
bed. If I was inside, I frequently relaxed in a high-backed
rocker with a patchwork cushion, wondering and dream-
ing about what it would be like when I grew up. Twilight
was a time for finding and listening to the world of
another kind of silence within. Where would I fit it?
What would I be doing? Would I be a writer like Jo in
Little Women? Jo—what a dashing name! Not like
Katie, which brought up images of *babushkas*, clogs, and
long skirts. Would I find someone to marry? I knew there
was another aspect of life, not often alluded to in our
home, but which I searched for in novels. It was connected with boys and love and romance.

Somehow someone had planted some seeds of
creativity in the fertile soil of this secret world, and
something told me to nourish those seedlings.

At the beginning of the 1940s I was ready to leave this
bifurcated existence and make my own way in life. I
thought I was ready. I had to be ready, for the end of
high school meant the end of living at home and being
supported by my father. I left Blaine Lake for the big
city. My name was Kay. My sisters gave me a gold
bracelet with "Kay" engraved on it. The other Katie living in Blaine Lake, a Russian girl, had also changed her
name—hers was now Katherine. My new name matched
the new image I developed for myself—pageboy haircut,
camel-hair coat with fox-fur collar, bright red lipstick,

high heels, and boyfriends. I felt I could safely shed the past.

I went to school. I worked. I married. I had several children. In the process I made some serious commitments to God as I knew and understood Him. And over a period of years Kay disappeared and Katie returned. I expected to spend the rest of my life safely isolated from society, like my mother had been, secure in my husband's love, caring for my children and home. I never saw myself in any other role and never suspected I might be forced to seek one. I never saw myself other than as a contented Mennonite wife and mother. Never middle-aged. Never alone.

Very soon I sensed a certain frustration and bitterness creeping in. As a single person, once the lipstick and high heels became less important than books and friends, I had become interested in all aspects of the work of the church and denomination I had worked for a while in a church college as secretary. Now, as a married woman, all of that except children's work in the local church, the sewing society, and musical activities was off limits. I saw myself walking in one door of the church and my husband in the other for the rest of my life, worshiping God from two angles. I was still Katie, a woman of peasant origins. I was not Kay or Katherine, or anything like that. I was doomed to be Katie, the Russian Mennonite maid, the rest of my life.

My childhood conditioning had caught up with me— not the church world across the river, but the world in our home, the world which began in Holland with Menno Simons and Conrad Grebel and continued to Germany, Prussia, Russia, and then to Canada; the world which over the years in Russia had determined the

identity and roles of all who became a part of it; the
world which found change hard to accept if it forced an
individual to accept new thinking. In this small world I
soon discovered that husbands were status symbols as
much as big cars and farms and that some women
received their sense of worth through the prominence of
their husbands in church activities. Could I find sufficient meaning in life as the wife of Walter Wiebe, a
young minister, without making any specific contribution to life on my own? Could Katie become a person?
Must she live her life as a Mennonite woman, waiting for
husband and children to come home to her to tell her
about their lives beyond the front gate, being glad when
they were glad, sad when they were sad? Could Katie
have no joy or sadness of her own?

Yet this situation wasn't unusual. Hundreds upon
hundreds of women had lived happily in this fashion. My
mother had had no other ambition in life but to be a
good wife and mother. But was this statement true?
What had she suffered in silence in the years before she
could speak the language of her neighbors, before she
could read English newspapers and even novels? Had
she never longed for something in addition to making
lemon pies, butter tarts, and knitted afghans? Why had I
never asked her? What made the agony even more
intense was that I felt guilty even questioning what
seemed right and pure: that a Mennonite woman named
Katie should never expect God to require anything more
of her than He had of her mother and of her mother
before her.

The harder I worked to fulfill my destiny to be Katie,
the more futile it seemed. I wanted desperately to serve
God and do what the church taught. I became increas-

ingly aware of the forces of church and society pushing
my husband and myself into two different directions, so
unlike our college experience when we'd had common
interests. Now we were members of the same church, but
he had first-class citizenship and I second-class. He went
to the policy-making meetings; Katie attended women's
meetings and mission rallies. He helped make decisions;
Katie served coffee and doughnuts. He studied the Word
of God; Katie sewed and hunted for bargains in clothing
and tracked down recipes and telephoned.

Was there no legitimate purpose for an education for a
Katie? What should I do with the longing to enjoy the
creativity of writing I had felt so many years ago as a
young girl? Must I say good-bye to that inner world of
the imagination I enjoyed while sitting in the rocker
waiting for Dad to come home from the store, or while
lying on the woodpile, warmed by the early spring sun? I
wondered. I agonized. Added to the pain was the
knowledge that my friends didn't understand that I
wanted to break loose from my immigrant bonds. I
wanted to leave the past behind. I wanted to quit being a
Mennonite.

One day I made my pilgrimage back to Blaine Lake, to
the house with the fence and gate, to the store with the
same wrinkled green shade.

You were out, Dad, but I saw your image behind the
counter, standing there in your sand-colored smock, adding up the day's receipts. I wanted to say, "Dad, you
made me a Mennonite when you gave me the name of
one. You had the chance here in Blaine Lake to pass us
off as Russians or Germans, but you didn't take it. You
loaded Mennonitism on us. You seduced me with your
stories of a people enduring pain and suffering for the

sake of their beliefs. I wanted to believe all of it. I wanted that faith that suffered hardship courageously and endured to the end. But now I find nothing but narrow authoritarianism and ecclesiastical pomposity out there. Dad, you escaped the bonds of the past by living here in Blaine Lake all these years. You could observe the situation from afar. But I've married into it. I can't get out. Dad, what do I do with this craving inside me to write— to wrap the experiences of the past in words and let others see what my life has been? Didn't you ever feel anything like that? You told us never to forget we were Funks. What did you mean by that?

"Why didn't you and Mother ever give me a real name? You called me Katie—a peasant name, not a writer's name, not a name for this land. And I have to use it all the time, exposing my past. You offered me the freedom of living in Blaine Lake, but at the same time wrapped a chain forged by your past experiences around me."

Dad, you weren't there in the store or in the warehouse or even in your tiny office at the back or in the basement with its stacks of canned goods and piles of empty cartons.

I left the store and walked down Main Street, past the dry-goods store owned by the village's only Jew, past the drugstore where we bought our medicine, past the cafe which once had a Chinese proprietor, around by the train station where we came and left so often during the war years, and then slowly down the other side, past the hotel, the pool hall, the hairdresser, the butcher shop, the other pool hall where we always slowed down to catch a glimpse of the sin that was supposed to be lurking in its dark corners, and past the bank with the benches in front on which sat the local unemployed and retired. Everything was nearly as it had been.

And I heard a voice whispering above the rattle and roar of cars and trucks looking for a parking spot: "I did give you a name, Katie, child of the prairies, child of the Russian steppes, child of many wanderings. But your name, being the gift of others, must be made your own. You didn't select your parents, your race, or your name, but you have to choose what you make of these experiences in Blaine Lake and the experiences of your parents and of their parents and of all those who searched for freedom of faith. Sometimes that search ended in failure for them. Sometimes it succeeded. It was a triumph of the spirit when those individuals accepted the gift of their heritage—the weaknesses, faults, mistakes, and the strengths, conquests, and joys—and gleaned from all what was needed to move ahead with courage."

Then I remembered one of your last letters, Dad. You wrote to me, "Yes, Katie, I made many mistakes in life. You only get experience after you have lived, but you need it before you live. And that is why a person makes mistakes. When I look back, I ask myself, why didn't I do it differently? Why didn't I? That is a question I can't answer. All I know is that I didn't have the experience to do it differently with the little education I had. Life is a struggle."

So you, too, sometimes wondered about the past.

As I walked down the last block, past the service station to turn toward the school, the dinginess of the community lifted and I could see it in a new way. *Life is a struggle, not a slippery slide.* The dirt road I remembered so well was now graveled. *Why didn't I do it differently?* The sign at the end of the street pointed the way to the highway. *You only get experience after you have lived.* And you gave me the experience, Dad, of reliving the past with you when you shared those memories with me.

I embraced my roots—the Mennonite ones and those grafted in by this variegated community in which I had lived almost eighteen years. My chains fell loose at my feet. My ancestors had not been complacent, accepting blindly what others told them to believe about God, life, and themselves. They had chosen. Mother and Dad had chosen a new way of living in a new country. That was their gift to me. I too could choose.

Other girls could be Kay, Kae, Katherine, Kathryn, Kathleen, Kaylene, and Kathy. I walked out of town bearing the name Katie proudly. It may have been the name of a peasant. But now it was my name.

Katie Funk Wiebe was born into a Russian Mennonite family in Saskatchewan in 1924. She is Assistant Professor of English at Tabor College, Hillsboro, Kansas, where she has taught since 1966.

Katie's incisive columns appear regularly in *Christian Leader, Gospel Herald, The Mennonite Brethren Herald,* and *The Mennonite.* She has also written for *Moody Monthly, Faith at Work, Festival Quarterly, Christian Living, With, Direction, Mennonite Weekly Review, Provident Book Finder,* and *Rejoice!*

The author is on the selection committee of Provident Readers Club, a member of the Peace Section of Mennonite Central Committee, literature coordinator of the Board of Christian Literature of the General Conference of Mennonite Brethren Churches, and active in other denominational assignments. She is a member of Parkview Mennonite Brethren Church in Hillsboro.

Mrs. Wiebe holds the MA degree from Wichita State University and the BA degree from Tabor College, both in English.